To the memory of
Felix and Gertrude Skoutajan

A Word About Names

Many places in the area of Europe that this story concerns saw place names change after the war. For instance until the end of the war, my home town was called the German, Aussig an der Elbe. Then after the explusion of the Germans, the name was changed to the Czech, Ústí nad labem. I have endeavoured to use the current (Czech) name when I write about contemporary events, and the original (German) name when I write about the time before the war.

UPROOTED AND
TRANSPLANTED

**A Sudeten Odyssey
From Tragedy to Freedom
1938 - 1958**

Hanns F. Skoutajan

The Ginger Press

Canadian Cataloguing in Publication Data

Skoutajan, Hanns, 1929-

Uprooted and Transplanted : a Sudeten odyssey from tragedy to freedom,
1938 - 1958

Includes bibliographical references.
ISBN 0-921773-54-4

1. Skoutajan, Hanns, 1929-   . 2. World War, 1939-1945 – Personal
narratives, Czech. 3. World War, 1939-1945 – Refugees – Biography.
4. World War, 1939-1945 – Czech Republic – Sudetenland. 5. Czechs –
Saskatchewan – Biography. 6. Czechs – Ontario – Batawa – Biography.
7. Czech Canadians – Biography.* 8. Batawa (Ont.) – Biography. I. Title.

D811.5.S56 2000   940.53'086'71   C00-932556-5

Cover photo: Sudeten refugees at Bright Sand, Saskatchewan, 1939

Design by Lori Ledingham

Published by
The Ginger Press, Inc.
848 Second Avenue East
Owen Sound, Ontario
Canada N4K 2H3

Printed in Canada.

CONTENTS

Kde domuv můj?
Where is my home?

The opening line of the Czech National Anthem

Preface

In September 1998, a small group of Canadians travelled to Munich, Germany, where they participated in a gathering to recall with sorrow the sixtieth anniversary of the Munich Agreement and its victims.

Following the ceremony, the group of Canadians along with some Germans travelled to places in the Czech Republic where they were born and from which they fled as political refugees after Hitler's army had taken over this predominantly German-speaking part of Czechoslovakia.

In 1938, after annexing Austria, Hitler demanded the Sudetenland–that region of Czechoslovakia which for over three centuries had been inhabited by ethnic Germans. Neville Chamberlain, the prime minister of Great Britain, under a bowler hat and carrying his tightly rolled umbrella, stepped off a plane in London waving a piece of paper and proclaiming, "peace with honour . . . peace in our time." The paper contained the words of a diplomatic compromise among Chamberlain, Hitler and the representatives of France and Italy (and without any Czech representatives) whereby the Sudetenland was ceded to the German Reich.

Many of the Sudetans sided with Hitler and welcomed

the German troops when they entered the area. There was, however, a significant number of Sudetens who stood in solidarity with the Czechs against Hitler and who became targeted for retaliation by the Nazis. These people suffered humiliation and death in Hitler's concentration camps and elsewhere. Some thirty-five thousand ethnic German antifascists did not manage to escape as my parents and I did, to Britain and then to Canada.

Even after the war, the Munich Agreement had dire consequences. Upon the liberation of Czechoslovakia at the war's end, three and a half million ethnic Germans were brutally mistreated, some were killed and virtually all were deprived of their citizenship and expelled from their homes by the newly liberated Czech government. It is against the backdrop of all these events that my story unfolds.

I have tried to tell the story of my family's flight from Sudentenland to Canada as I experienced it in my youth. The dramatic events of that time had a profound impact on me. This is a story that I wish to share with the people in my adoptive homeland who may have only vague notions of what transpired in central Europe before, during and after the Second World War.

These historic events have also deeply affected my spiritual journey and my understanding of the Judeo-Christian faith. It is my hope that *Uprooted and Transplanted* will help Canadians and others observe the events of this time and become aware of the subtle changes that are threatening the democratic system of which we are so proud. Hopefully, my story will show how people of faith can play a role in opposing those malignant "principalities and powers."

Pastor Martin Niemoeller, a German who lived and suffered through the Nazi era, wrote:

First, they arrested the Communists. But I was not a Communist, so I did nothing.

Then, they came for the Social Democrats. But I was not a Social Democrat, so I did nothing.

Then they arrested the trade unionists. And I did nothing because I was not one.

And then they came for the Jews and then the Catholics. But I was neither a Jew nor a Catholic and I did nothing.

At last they came and arrested me. And there was no one left to do anything about it.

Pastor Niemoeller's own bitter experience is reflected in these words. You might want to add your own groups to his litany.

Rather than writing an academic examination of the political and historic events during this turbulent period, I have chosen to tell this story as a childhood memory, as recollections of a student of theology, and as a pastor and church leader.

I am indebted to so many people, particularly: Dr. Bob and Stella Weil of Halifax, who encouraged me in this project; many members of my extended family; Sudetens in Canada and Germany; but most of all to my parents, Felix and Gertrude Skoutajan, whose political convictions and spirituality were intimately bound together, and who indeed "fought the good fight."

Finally, I wrote these words in the hope that my daughter, Karla, and son, Stephen, will live their lives in a more peaceful and just society.

Hanns Skoutajan
November 2000

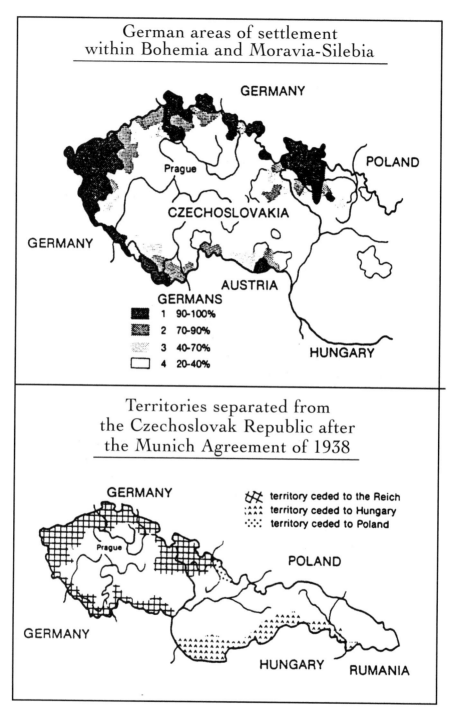

German areas of settlement within Bohemia and Moravia-Silebia

GERMANY

POLAND

Prague

CZECHOSLOVAKIA

GERMANY

AUSTRIA

GERMANS
1 90-100%
2 70-90%
3 40-70%
4 20-40%

HUNGARY

Territories separated from the Czechoslovak Republic after the Munich Agreement of 1938

GERMANY

⊞ territory ceded to the Reich
⋮ territory ceded to Hungary
⋮ territory ceded to Poland

Prague

POLAND

GERMANY

HUNGARY   RUMANIA

CHAPTER ONE

Towards
A Further Shore

The Elbe River near Aussig

Towards
A Further Shore

Tell the Israelites to go forward.
Exodus 14:15

A large crowd had gathered at the seashore. They stood at the very edge of the water gazing worriedly at the horizon. Their heads turned nervously to look over their shoulders. In the distance a cloud of dust was rising, indicating a pursuing force. Their leader was urging them to enter the water and to flee across. The Sea of Reeds was just that, not terribly deep but wide enough that the further shore could scarcely be seen. It was risky to be sure, but what was the alternative, to be caught, slaughtered or returned to slavery in the brick kilns of Egypt and punished with even harsher enforcements?

Finally one ventured into the water. A breeze rippled the surface. Wavelets formed, grew larger. The water shifted away from the shore like a receding tide. The man who had dared to take the first step into the sea now found that he stood on dry ground. He took another step and again the water moved away, then another and another, with the same result. The rest of the crowd saw what was happening and began to follow him. The water seemed to part before them, the reeds bending to form a carpet on which to walk. At length the most doubting among them set foot on the seabed. Looking behind them, they could see the dust cloud approaching. Dark figures of horses and riders and chariots became visible. The most cautious of the escapees needed no further encouragement. They rushed into the sea in search of freedom.

I'm not sure whether the biblical Exodus was quite like that, at least that's how it appears to my imagination. Somehow the Israelites escaped from Egypt. How many we do not know; however, a whole race that eventually became scattered across the entire world looks back to this event as the birthing of their nation. It began with a venture for liberation, an Exodus.

Centuries later their descendants, a real nation with a king, capital and temple, were defeated. The slaughter was great and those who did not die in battle were harnessed and marched out of their once promised land. The trek was long and hard. Many died before they reached Babylon. The strong survived only to become slaves. A generation later they still remembered their homeland which now lay in ruins. The temple, the walls of the city, all lay in shambles. The wind blew sand across the land. A few survivors tended their sheep among the debris of that former civilization. In distant Babylon the exiles wept. Their masters demanded that they sing songs of Zion. "How can we?" they asked.

Eventually, when the tide of history changed some returned and struggled to rebuild what was lost. But many others remained behind or wandered off to other places. God's proud people were dispersed and today centuries later, can be found on every continent. Nevertheless they look back to the old homeland with great reverence. Israel remains the spiritual home of every Jew.

      ✿   ✿   ✿

On the wall of our family room hangs an original oil painting of the valley of the Elbe River near Czernosek in what is now the Czech Republic, an area well known for its vineyards. It is a beautiful picture that reminds me of my homeland. When it was painted the inhabitants of that area were mostly German. All that has changed. I cannot help but wonder whether another generation will remember the Elbe valley, the Bohemian forest, the Moravian country-side, cities such as Olmuetz, Karlsbad and Aussig, the city where I was born.

The German population left under duress. That is not new in the history of the world. Indeed the account of humanity is that of wandering, settling, disruption and re-establishment. Each family and clan has its own story. What I have written is not a political analysis or an effort to lay blame or demand restitution. Nor have I any intention to return to my homeland and my children certainly have no desire to reclaim the land I left behind. But stories must be preserved and so I have set down these memories first of all for them but also for anyone who may be curious enough to read about it.

CHAPTER TWO

Springtime in Prague

Prague with Hradčany Castle in the background

Springtime in Prague

Going home, going home, I am going home
American folk song

The train rattled over the switches as it moved out of the old and dirty railway station of the city of Dresden. Even so many years after the end of the war, the ravages of the saturation bombing were still visible. Here and there throughout the city, brick enclosures held rocks and concrete pieces and other debris that were once homes, churches, office buildings and stores. These were replaced by large, nondescript edifices that were completely out of style with the beautiful old baroque architecture of what remained of this once proud centre of culture. Cranes dotted the urban skyline.

Soon the city was left behind and so were the reminders of the war. The flatness of East Germany gave way to wooded hills through which the Elbe River wound its way. Old paddlewheel steamers belching black smoke struggled against the current of the river which was now being squeezed between steep hills.

It was the spring of 1968 and I was returning to the land of my birth for the first time in thirty years. I was travelling to Prague by train with a group of American Methodists to attend the fourth Christian Peace Conference. We had been visiting in the German Democratic Republic (GDR) which was in turmoil over the events taking place in neighbouring Czechoslovakia where Alexander Dubček was making big changes, calling for "socialism with a human face." Among the communists in the GDR there was fear that the virus might be transmitted. We heard of factory, community and school meetings where leaders were criticizing the reforms of the Czechs. Signs on billboards, usually long complicated sentences full of political jargon, denounced the changes in their neighbouring country and vouched faithfulness to their "friends" in the Soviet Union. Privately the East Germans expressed some envy.

We noticed the difference at the Czech-German border. As the train pulled out of Bad Schandau, the last station in the GDR, the Czech officials began their passport inspection. There were two of them: one was an elderly jolly person who smiled a lot and welcomed us with whatever English he had at his command; the other was a rather stout and officious looking woman who didn't smile at all. It seemed like the new and the old orders were very much with us on that train as we entered Czech territory. We were heading into the Prague Spring.

The rail line followed the Elbe River which snakes its way through the beautiful sandstone mountains known as the Saxonian Alps. Our first stop after crossing the frontier was the city of Děčin where we all rushed out to change our money at the foreign exchange booth on the railway platform. I had never been to Děčin although it was only a short distance from Aussig where I had lived for the first nine years of my life. In the days before the war it had been two cities, Tetschen and Bodenbach. Some of my best friends had come from these twin cities situated across the Elbe River from each other. They were mainly German communities boasting a strong anti-fascist movement in the days before the 1938 Munich Agreement severed this city as well as the rest of the Sudetenland from Czechoslovakia. Whenever there was a political rally, the people of Tetschen and Bodenbach were always well represented.

Soon I would be passing through the city of my birth. The train continued to follow the river. I observed the familiar barge traffic on the Elbe that I had often watched from the banks with my mother. As the train slowed, my heart began to race. My American companions sensed my excitement and watched me with interest. I had told some of them about my flight from this country thirty years earlier and that this was my first homecoming. Unfortunately their understanding of the history of central Europe was very limited and, although they had heard about the Munich Agreement, its impact on this small nation was not comprehended. Prime Minister Neville Chamberlain had described Czechoslovakia as "a far away country inhabited by quarrelling people of whom we know nothing." Certainly the aftermath, the expulsion of the Sudeten Germans, was unknown to my fellow passengers and, indeed, to most people with whom I have discussed this subject.

My first glimpse of Aussig, now Ústí nad labem, was the Dr. Eduard Beneš Bridge, the "new bridge" as it was then known. I remembered when it was built. I had been at its dedication, in which my father had participated, and was one of the first to walk across to the neighbouring city of Schreckenstein. I also recalled having had pointed out to me the containers for explosives attached underneath it in preparation for a German attack and had wondered why such a new and beautiful bridge should be fitted with the means for its own destruction.

In Ústí nad labem, its Czech name on the sign board with "Aussig" in brackets underneath, the train came to a brief halt. From my train window I saw the tower of the Catholic church, the "Stadtkirche" where my mother had been baptized and confirmed. In the square beside the church, a fish market was held each Friday, and it was here we bought the fish for our special Christmas Eve dinner, an event I still fondly remember. The carp was often still thrashing around in our basket as we walked away. The tower of the church now stands at a rakish angle, tilted by a bomb which fell nearby in the last days of the war. Next to the Tower of Pisa, the Stadtkirche is the most gravity defying structure in the northern hemisphere, so a tour guidebook informed me. It remains that way even now, more than fifty years after the end of hostilities. The tower was symbolic of much in that city, transformed as it was by the war and its immediate aftermath: the expulsion of 80 percent of the population, almost 95 percent of the German citizens. Although Aussig was still familiar to me, it was also very different, as I found out later in the week when I returned for a one-day visit.

I looked at the worn and cracked concrete of the railway platform and wondered whether I had in fact stood on that very surface when mother and I left early that October morning in 1938. Thirty years of history had wrought many physical as well as human changes. I hurried back and forth from window to window across the coach to take in as much as I could. My mind was swept by a rush of memories and questions as I recognized familiar scenes.

The train once again began to move, passing over the Bíla, a small river that merges with the Elbe. It had always been a terribly polluted stream coming out of the heart of the industrial and brown coal mining area. On the other side high above the bank and the power dam that harnessed the Elbe River stood the castle Schreckenstein, like a sentinel overlooking the river in both directions. Hundreds of years ago, it had been a toll station. The Elbe, like the Rhein and the Danube, had been a highway of commerce and traders were halted below the castle where duties were collected. As a child I knew it as an historic ruin with a restaurant at the top, a place for hiking excursions. For us children it was exciting to go up to the turret of the castle high above the river and peer through the barred door to see several armoured manikins. A coin dropped into a slot caused these figures to move and rattle their chain-mail armour frighteningly which always gave us a thrill.

From its first settlement nine hundred years ago, the people of Aussig were German and over its entire history until the end of the Second World War in 1945 it had remained so. The *Vertreibung* (expulsion or ethnic cleansing) changed all that. The German citizens of Aussig were part of the three and a half million who were driven from their homes by the liberated Czechs. At this terrible time, Germans from many parts of Europe that had been under Nazi control were driven from their homes. Aussig has seen much pain and suffering over its lifetime, particularly during those days immediately after the war's end. The Germans were replaced mostly by Slovaks and gypsies, people often not familiar with city living. Many of them stayed only a short time before trying to return to a more familiar way of life.

It was getting dark as the train proceeded up the river valley. I noticed the names of the stations had been changed to Czech on the billboards. My colleagues plied me with lots of questions about what we had seen. None of them had ever heard of the mass expulsions that had changed this country so drastically.

Two hours later the train entered the city of Prague. The red light still glowed on the radio beacon on the hill near the castle. Thirty years ago, as a child, it was this light I had watched disappear, craning my neck as we travelled east towards Poland on the refugee train. It now seemed like an old friend.

Our train came to a hissing halt at what used to be called Masaryk station after the first president of

13

Czechoslovakia. Each new government had changed its name. When we walked down the platform I noticed that it was called simply Central Station. Now, however, its old name has been restored. We were taken to the Park Hotel, a modern, comfortable place constructed for foreign visitors. We were to spend the week here while attending the Christian Peace Conference at the nearby exhibition grounds.

The next morning we woke to a beautiful spring day. It was Sunday and a group of us decided to go for a walk along the Vlatva (Moldau) River bank toward the centre of the city. We soon became aware of the Prague Spring. The icy facade of orthodox communism was cracking up. Pictures of Masaryk appeared in the windows. The people we encountered were very friendly, some greeted us in English. It seemed they had breathed fresh air. We came to a Catholic church where a mass was in progress. We went in and stood at the back and watched as the worshippers moved forward to the altar to receive communion. A Czech hymn was being sung. There was something wonderfully familiar to me in the sound of the words and the typically Czech melody. My eyes filled with tears and I sensed weakness in my knees. I leaned against a pillar. My friends seemed to understand and perhaps even felt a certain personal involvement in my feelings. I didn't need to explain that somehow I felt I was home. Although I couldn't understand the language nevertheless everything had a strange familiarity. No, that's not an oxymoron!

We crossed one of the many bridges spanning the Moldau and walked through the narrow alleyways toward the centre of the city to the famous Wenzeslaus Square with its statue of the saint in armour, sitting astride a horse. This famous place is not so much a square as a broad avenue with a wide boulevard down the centre, a kind of Champs Élysée. It is the place to which demonstrators are drawn as they were when Russian tanks put an end to the Prague

Spring and where Jan Palach immolated himself in protest against the invasion. It is also the place where Václav Havel, who had just recently come out of prison, addressed the people at the time of the Velvet Revolution when communism came to its end.

Later on, at a stall on the old city square near the famous astrological clock, I bought coloured Easter eggs to take home with me to Canada. Every year at Easter, I unpack them and make them the centrepiece of our coffee table. We crossed the river again, this time by way of the celebrated Charles Bridge which was constructed by Emperor Charles IV in the fourteenth century. History is everywhere in this city. I was less interested in the Peace Conference than in simply breathing in the spirit of a newly liberated Prague that I had left at its darkest hour. Could this liberation continue? We could not see how it might be stopped.

On Thursday of that week I had to make a difficult decision: would I go to Lidice with my companions or return to my birthplace, Aussig? Lidice, once a small community near Prague, is now a memorial to Nazi savagery. It was here that all male residents were executed in retaliation for the assassination of Reinhard Heydrich, the Nazi commander of Prague. Much of the wrath of the post-war government of Czechoslovakia against the Germans was brought about by the memory of this atrocity. My decision was the more personal one and so I took the bus to Aussig.

On the way I recognized the very place on the road between Terecin and Lovosice where mother and I had crossed the provisional border that separated the Sudetenland from Czechoslovakia after the German takeover.

I had some relatives in Aussig and had telegraphed them, personal telephones still being quite rare, to ask them to meet me at the bus terminal. What I had neglected to say was that I meant the bus terminal in Aussig, thus no one was there to meet me. I waited for over half an hour and then decided to set out on my own. This was propitious inasmuch as I had the city with all its memories to myself. I walked for more than three hours.

My sentimental tour took me past the place where my grandmother had lived, a place I had visited weekly. The baroque opera house where my father had been on the board of management announced that evening's concert, Smetana's "Ma Vlast" (My Fatherland). How appropriate the invitation seemed. I walked slowly through the city park hoping to find that big rock where I was photographed as a five year old but sadly didn't find it. I saw my father's office building and the *Volkshaus* (People's House) where the Sudeten Social Democrats had their office and where they gathered to talk and plan over mugs of beer. I then set out for the suburb where I had lived, an area rich in childhood memories, passing on the way the maternity home where I was born. As I neared the place where I had spent the first nine years of my life, I was almost afraid to look; but inevitably I came to The Star, a place where a number of streets converged, and from which I could see my former home. Slowly, I walked down Karl Marx Street to number 43. I was taking lots of photos and have one of the apartment house as seen from this vantage point. On closer inspection I found the place looking rather dismal. The plaster was dirty gray and cracked. Nevertheless, those three windows on the top floor sent a lump to my throat.

I walked up the side street in order to look into the garden where I used to play and was about to take a picture when a woman approached. She whispered in German, "But that's not a very pretty scene." She said it so softly that I might not have taken notice had it not been in my mother tongue in this place where German is seldom spoken in public. As I lowered my camera I heard her continue, "but perhaps it was home." I nodded and suddenly she began to weep. At length she started to tell me her own story. She had come from another city and had not experienced the terrible events in Aussig but of course knew the bitter story. I told her a bit about myself but soon we began to realize that we had attracted some attention. Curtains in the windows of nearby houses moved suspiciously. My acquaintance seemed worried and quickly bade farewell and went on her way. I discovered in my brief sojourn in Aussig that the thaw of the Prague Spring had not reached far beyond the capital. The new freedom seemed fragile still.

I continued my walk to the suburb where my relatives lived. Everything was so familiar, I even found the shortcut where, as a child, I had to cross a brook by means of a set of stepping stones. The stones were much closer together than in my memories. I reached the house where my aunt, uncle and cousin had lived. They had been among those driven out, but because of their anti-fascist credentials they were able to turn the house over to the present occupants, also relatives, who were able to remain there.

Shortly after my arrival at the house, my relatives returned from Prague where they had gone expecting to meet me at the bus terminal. In spite of this misunderstanding and the long drive they had taken, I was royally welcomed. They had a car and took me to other parts of the city I had not yet seen. Best of all they took me to what had once been our summer cottage, now a dilapidated shack that bore no resemblance to anything I could recall. Over a supper of sauerbraten and dumplings we told our stories. Later on they drove me back to Prague where I was expected to attend a meeting.

There is one other event that I must relate of this first return visit. Our group was to fly to Moscow on Saturday afternoon. On that last morning in Prague, I decided to make a brief visit to the Canadian embassy. I found my way and met Peg Smith of the Canadian YWCA who had also been to the Peace Conference. We both arrived at the embassy gates at the same time. Before going in she told me the terrible news of the assassination of Martin Luther King. That news was instantly everywhere. It cast a dark cloud over my travelling companions, some of whom had known King personally and had walked with him at Selma, Alabama. It drew a shroud over all of Prague. The question presented itself: could the Prague Spring come to full and lasting flower in a world where prophets are still murdered even in democratic U.S.A?

The Prague Spring came and went and with it the brief experiment in socialism with a human face. Alexander Dubček disappeared from view and the Moldau froze over once again. Had it only been a "winter born," a false thaw? Did the Hussite warriors of long ago emerge briefly from their hiding place in the White Mountain as folklore has it and then retreat again until a more opportune time? It would take another twenty years.

In 1993, three years after the Velvet Revolution, Marlene, my spouse, and I returned to Prague and Aussig. In the sunshine the city looked beautiful and I was able to show her the many places familiar from my childhood. The old apartment house had a new coat of stucco and was painted to look almost new. The trees in the park looked green and healthy although this is one of the most polluted places in the world. Downtown on market square we found a restaurant with a German menu on a board outside. Our waiter spoke to us in German and made me feel somewhat at home.

Heraclitus the Greek philosopher of antiquity once said, "You can't cross the same river twice," it is never the same river. Neither is the Moldau or the Elbe, everything has changed and so have we. I still recall what I saw with the eyes of a child and can tell the stories of those youthful days. It's important to share them, but I doubt whether any words can convey the feelings that I experience even as I recount my memories. Much in these stories is bound up with people who are gone, expelled as the liberated Czechoslovakia sought to "cleanse" itself of a non-Czech element. Others–uncles, aunts, cousins and friends–were killed in the war or have died since. It is never the same. Spring and autumn come and pass away.

CHAPTER THREE

What's in a Name?

Felix Skoutajan with his mother, Rosa
circa 1901

What's in a Name?

Who has not own'd with rapture smitten fame,
The Power of grace, the magic of a name?
Thomas Campbell: Pleasant Home, 1799

"Skoutajan—what kind of name is that?" This is a question I have often been asked. Does this story follow a myth or history? Or are history and myth always so intertwined that they are inseparable? I had a professor of history who explained to the class that anything beyond a hundred years ago and often sooner is mythology. That, of course, does not mean "untrue." What it means is that true history is more than facts and dates. Real history can only be conveyed by stories which may not be factually accurate but nevertheless reflect the truth more completely than mere fact. Does this make sense? I hope my story does. Please don't ask whether it is true!

Our family's story of our ancestors' origins takes us back three turbulent centuries to a time quite unlike our own which, nevertheless, has a profound significance for me. I have never been to the area where my ancestors lived although I have now seen a picture of the little hamlet in the hills of central Moravia. A friend of mine took it but was unable to find any record of my family. It may be due to the fact that documents were destroyed by a fire in the church that is central to my story. The little village doesn't look like anything I have in my imagination. The modern world has made its impact, urbanization has played havoc with the picture in my mind. Allow me now to let imagination have its reign.

In my mind's eye, I see a little community in a narrow valley with many oak trees. A rutted road leads through it and winds its way back out over the hills on its way north-ward to the city of Olmuetz. At the bottom of the valley the road runs over a stone bridge and then between a few hous-es. There is, of course, the local tavern and guest house where travellers can stay overnight. Behind it is a yard with a stable where stage coaches change their teams. The church dominates the little valley, its steeple thrusting out above the trees. Adjacent to the cemetery that undoubtedly gives rest to the bones of ancestors of mine, is a rather large rectory where an ancient priest is looked after by a house-keeper. There is one other person living in the rectory, a young priest who has been sent to relieve the old man who can scarcely get around, let alone stand up long enough to say mass.

The young man, Father Florian, has been in the com-munity for a little over a year. People still find it hard to call him "father" inasmuch as he is so much younger than the old man he has come to assist. If the old man was, indeed, "Father," Florian could only be a son.

Early one Sunday morning Florian made his way to the church to celebrate mass. It was still dark; the church in the valley did not get sunlight until later in the morning. Florian stumbled along the path from the back of the rec-tory, past the cemetery. Just as he rounded the corner of the church he saw something lying in his way. He almost tripped on it. It looked like a bundle of rags.

Florian stopped and wondered whether he should just

step around it and continue on to the front steps of the church. Then he recalled a warning he had received the night before while hearing confessions. The words had bothered him until he finally fell asleep. He had forgotten them in the morning but now they resurfaced. "Look out at the corner," a penitent had said before retreating from the confessional in a great hurry.

These confessionals were usually very boring and Florian listened to them only halfheartedly. At first he had been very diligent; indeed, even now he tried to live up to his vows, tried to listen in a caring way and suggest more than just rote repetitions of prayers before granting absolution. But after hearing a dozen or so, all of which seemed to be much the same–a recitation of petty sins, looking lustfully or even acting so, stealing someone's goose from the commons "by mistake," having an extra at the tavern without paying–he had become lax. It had occurred to him that Jesus or Mary would have yawned as well.

However, when a young woman's voice said these words, "Look out for the corner," he was startled to attention but not fast enough. Before he pulled aside the curtain, the sound of the steps was fading away. The heavy door slammed shut. She had started her confession with the usual formula, "Father, I have sinned" and suddenly stopped, blurted out those few words and then retreated hastily.

Now this bundle of blankets just at this corner of the church confronted him. Florian stooped to examine the object and quickly discovered that it wasn't just blankets. It moved, it gave a little cry. It was a baby, a very new baby at that and very much alive.

Florian picked it up, looked around to see whether anyone had observed him but no one was yet on their way to the church. "What now?" he wondered. As a priest he knew very well what needed to be done–the baby must be baptized lest its life journey proves short; unbaptized, it would be consigned to limbo. The responsibility was upon him to make sure that this life was not lost to the world or the realm of the blessed beyond.

He picked up the bundle and hurried into the church where two women were kneeling in prayer. At the sacristy door stood his housekeeper. Holding the bundle in his arms he motioned to her to follow him. Foundlings were not unusual. There were lots of unwanted babies, mostly illegitimate offspring, that the church had to care for somehow. Bošena, who was not just housekeeper but also acted as caretaker of the small church, had the altar prepared. Florian unwrapped the bundle to see the small child, which he discovered to be a male, and then carried him to the back of the church where the font was located in a little alcove off the entryway.

"In the name of the Father and the Son and the Holy Spirit," he paused; what would he call this bit of life? All he knew was its sex. He would have to give it some sort of name. "Jan" or John came to his mind immediately, John from the corner, would distinguish him from the many other Johns or Jans in the village. The so-called "emergency baptism" was quickly accomplished. The water splattered on his head roused this little life and his cries filled the church. The two praying women came out of their pious poses and craned their necks to see what was happening. By this time several other villagers had taken their places and more were proceeding into the sanctuary. Bošena took the baby out of his arms and Florian rushed into the sacristy to don his robe.

What a way to start the day! During mass, his mind kept slipping from his task. Again and again he heard the young woman's voice in the confessional. He tried to identify it. It was not unfamiliar.

"Jan Skouta," John from the corner. The name stuck.

The old priest cradled him like a great grandchild. Bošena cared for him like a mother, a grandmother, perhaps.

Young Father Florian was filled with penitent thoughts. He had entered the priesthood with all good and noble intentions, but he was a human, a male human at that, with all its urges and temptations, and of course, human weaknesses. He heard about such weaknesses in the confessional and although he handed out "stiff" sentences he could not help but feel Mary smile understandingly on such human conditions. After all she too was a human, although the Christian church had virtually turned her into God. Mother of God, could that be more than God?

In his private meditations Florian had wondered about the Virgin. "Young woman" it meant. He had fantasized about her and then felt guilty. Where did her baby come from? From the Holy Spirit, of course, who had had his way with her. "Having his way," Florian wondered about this phrase and felt the temptation surge up in him. Fingering his beads passionately helped temporarily but sooner or later that warm feeling in his groin emerged again.

He dreamed, or was it a dream, that he encountered a peasant girl who looked on him and saw his maleness thinly covered by his priesthood. They met secretly, passionately. It all happened so fast. Was it the action of the Holy Spirit? If God had sent his spirit to a young woman, could it be that God could also send his spirit through a man? Was sex then a holy act? The act was brief but never confessed, rather repressed, to be remembered in embarrassing dreams. Was Jan Skouta a child of the spirit?

Within the year the old priest died. Bošena brought her daughter Marguerite to help her with her duties around the house and in the church. The younger woman also took charge of baby Jan and tended him like a mother. There were whisperings about the village, especially in the tavern,

27

where the human aspects of the priesthood were often hinted at. "Holy Family" some snickered and all understood.

"He grew up in wisdom, stature and in favour with God and man," and so did Jan. Florian or Father Florian as he finally became known proved to be a good priest, beloved by his people, beloved also by God, for when a "sickness" invaded this small community sending many to their deaths, Florian accepted his duties conscientiously and God rewarded him, sending him to "his mother's arms."

And so my story of Florian ends and the story of a name begins. It began at a corner, a church corner. Jan, Johannus, Ian, Ionas, Giovanni, Hans or John, they are universal names, in whatever corner they are found.

CHAPTER FOUR

Full Circle

The author's son, Stephen, in front of
33 Arbeitergasse in Vienna where
Stephen's grandfather, Felix, was born in 1901

Full Circle

Vienna, city of my dreams
Johann Strauss

"Your father was a child of love," Aunt Helene confided to me over a cup of Kafe mit Schlag as we sat in one of Vienna's famous Kafehauses. Helene isn't a real aunt of mine, our relationship is a bit more distant than that. She belongs to the part of the family that remained in this city that was once the glittering capital of the Hapsburg empire. She was a real Viennese, a lover of life, of good food and music, and was deeply in love with this city and its rich culture. Her husband was a forestry expert and dean of the Polytechnical Institute of Vienna.

It was in the spring of 1957 when I made my first visit to Vienna. I had been studying at a university in northern Germany, in a setting that could hardly be more different from where I now found myself, where nevertheless the same language was spoken although with a distinctly different accent. At the end of my first semester, I had bought a used Volkswagen and on the first day of my holidays took off for this city that I had heard so much about from my parents.

I had no contact with the Viennese branch of the

Skoutajan family; indeed, I did not know if there were any left. After the turbulent times, when my father left as a small child with his mother, Rosa, it was difficult to know if any of our relatives were still alive.

On arrival I settled myself in a rather expensive hotel room. Vienna was crowded with Hungarians who had fled the abortive uprising in the fall of 1956. Although the exchange rate for the Canadian dollar was great, the room was still above what a student could afford. I was disappointed. The weather was dull and damp. I had discovered that "Die Walkuere," one of my favourite operas, was playing at the State Opera but it was already sold out. I felt very much alone. Sitting in my overpriced hotel room, I turned to the telephone directory to look for a namesake. Lo and behold there was one, a Paula Skoutajan. I was excited but a bit hesitant to pick up the phone and dial the number.

When I finally did ring I heard the voice of an elderly woman on the line. I identified myself as a Skoutajan, son of Felix, a theological student from Canada in search of relatives. She listened and then amazed me, "I know who your father is, I am his grand aunt." Next thing I knew I had accepted an invitation to supper at her apartment which turned out to be but a short distance from the hotel where I was now staying.

I was indeed excited. Her accent was familiar to me. She sounded very much like my father did whenever he spoke with someone from this city or recited some poem or the words of a Viennese song such as *Wannɔ Bleulueftl ɔeufzlt*. (That's untranslatable.)

The following evening armed with a bottle of wine and a small bouquet of flowers, I made my way to the address she had given me. Presently I found the large old apartment house which had an arched gateway leading through the building into a courtyard. In days gone by it had probably been used as a passage for coaches. It was quite dark by now and the archway was lit by a very dim light. The door into the apartment house opened from the interior of this entryway.

As I hesitated in front of the door, a figure moved out of the shadows and grabbed me by my arm. "Who are you?" a male voice demanded. I quickly declared my name and intention and immediately the hold relaxed.

"My name is Rudolf," he now introduced himself. "You are not Herbert are you?" A few months earlier my father's youngest and only surviving brother had gone missing, the result of an amnesia attack it was surmised. He had not yet been found and the incident had received a good deal of publicity. Obviously the Viennese Skoutajans were some-what concerned that I might be this person and perhaps deranged and dangerous.

Rudolf was now satisfied that I was not Herbert but his nephew, Felix's son from Canada and therefore a benign visitor. He introduced himself as Paula's son and escorted me up several flights of stairs to a door with the name "Paula Skoutajan" on it. It gave me quite a jolt to see my surname in a place so totally unfamiliar. This is an experi-ence that Smiths in anglophone countries or Schmidts in Germany won't experience. With one of those large old-fashioned keys he opened the door for me and I beheld a very old woman with snow white hair drawn tightly on top of her head. She was short and heavily built, somewhat severe at first glance. She spread out her arms to me and drew me to her. *Recht herzlich wilkommen in deiner Heimat Stadt* (Welcome into your home town), she greeted me. Rudolf now stood by with a slight smile. I presented my flowers and wine and was escorted into the room where a dining table was all set out for the three of us.

What followed was an exciting evening of instruction in family history, much of which I had not known. A drawer was opened and pictures brought out, some of them old daguerreotypes, brownish in colour, of family members. Among them was a family portrait, in the middle of which was a woman with a small baby. That child was Felix, my father, sitting in his mother's lap. The picture was not unfamiliar. I had a vague recollection of having seen this photo before, probably back in Czechoslovakia many years earlier.

Later that evening, the doorbell rang and a woman in her sixties entered. I was introduced to Aunt Helene, Rudolf's sister. News of my arrival had travelled quickly. She was now to take charge of my visit to Vienna, to take me sightseeing while Rudolf organized a family evening at a Heuriger party in Grinzing, the famous new wine suburb. We drank wine carefully, as my relatives wise to the power of this beverage instructed me. We listened to the accordion player who came to our table and played and sang songs, some of which Rudolf had composed. Many other relatives with different names were introduced to me. I discovered a new family. Paula insisted I quit my expensive hotel and move into her spare bedroom. I was "home" after all. Not only that but when they heard about my bad luck with the State Opera, I was told they knew the manager and I would get a ticket. The sun also began to shine.

The reason I did not locate Rudolf in the phone book was that he had dropped the "O" from our name and was now listed as "Skutajan." He was a composer of popular songs, a civil wedding magistrate in one of Vienna's districts and a frequenter of the casino in the Wienerwald. He has, however, always remained a bit of a mysterious character. I met both his wife and their son.

It was the following day that Helene and I met at the Kafehaus where she informed me that my father was "a child of love," born "out of wedlock" in other words. That wasn't much of a problem in the sophisticated society of the capital of the Austro-Hungarian empire where nobility and

Full Circle

creative people led unorthodox lives. No one called my father a little bastard. Indeed, Father had been predeceased by two older siblings before he was born. Joseph, my grandfather, was a signals engineer on the Imperial Austrian Railways and moved about the empire frequently while Rosa Zesula, my grandmother, continued to live in Vienna. It just hadn't been convenient for Joseph and Rosa to legalize their union. Thus father's birth and baptism certificates list him as Felix Zesula.

Little is known about Rosa's family background. She was, however, a typical Viennese woman, in love with life and her city. Her name indicates that her ancestors, like those of her husband, came from the province of Moravia, now the Czech Republic.

Bohemia and Moravia were part of the Austro-Hungarian empire. Many years earlier these had been independent nations with a proud heritage. The Skoutajans came from a part of Moravia that was home to a large German speaking minority. Brno, the capital, was virtually a bilingual city.

At the time of my father's birth in 1901, Joseph Skoutajan had been working in Aussig, an important rail centre in Bohemia. When this position became a permanent placement for him, Rosa and Joseph were married and took up residence in Aussig on the Elbe, in a large apartment on the main street which they soon populated with three more boys and one girl.

At the end of the First World War, the old empire was dismembered into a number of smaller states. On 28 October 1918, Czechoslovakia became an independent state with Prague as its beautiful and historic capital. It was a city familiar to Mozart and Dvořak and once upon a time, it had been capital of the Holy Roman Empire.

Although Austro-Hungary is generally regarded as having been an aristocratic empire, a strong social democratic

35

movement had developed among its working class citizens. Grandfathers of mine had paraded proudly in the May Day celebrations in Vienna, a red carnation in their lapels. This labour movement had worked hard for a liberal democracy and when the empire was broken up their unity was splintered into a number of countries. Nevertheless these social democrats maintained a strong sense of allegiance. They felt drawn to their compatriots in the new Austria. I recall my parents attending rallies in Vienna. Now their task was to continue to struggle for the same ideals in their various new nations where they found themselves. More than that they pressed for some measure of autonomy for those German people who had lived in Bohemia and Moravia for over seven hundred years.

The new Czech government wanted to celebrate their liberty from their old Austro-German oppressors. Ancient and modern scores continued to be remembered. The scene was thus set for the struggle that pitted Germans against Czechs, but also Germans against Germans in this fledgling state in the very heart of Europe.

In the mid-1920s, neighbouring Germany was gradually recovering from the embarrassment foisted upon it by the Treaty of Versailles. As well, the economic depression that was felt all around the world devastated Germany and set the stage for a takeover by a demagogue who spoke with powerful charisma about "the great destiny of the German people." In the early 1930s, Hitler and his thugs, an ultra-nationalistic and conservative force that found the Jews a convenient target for every ailment of the people, particularly the economy, came to power. By the end of the Second World War, they had murdered six million Jews throughout Europe. Eighty thousand Czech and Moravian Jews perished in the Holocaust.

At first Hitler had planned simply to drive out the Jewish people from Germany. Many of them had only the slightest consciousness of their Jewishness. They had thought themselves to be just plain German, Austrian, Hungarian or Czech. Many of them had hoped to remain and weather out the storm, to wait out this "passing insanity" until better times. Others found nowhere to go. Whole boatloads of Jews, such as those on the St. Louis, sailed from port to port in Canada and the United States only to be rejected and finally returned to Germany and extermination camps. Indeed, we Canadians have a stake in the Holocaust. Palestine, the ancient homeland of the Hebrews, was the hoped for destination of many but this British protectorate refused to allow them to enter in large numbers.

Hitler grew more ambitious. He played on the pride of Germans beyond his borders, especially in those countries of the old Austro-Hungarian empire. First of all he demanded the *Anschluss* (annexation) of Austria which took place in March of 1938. German troops were jubilantly welcomed in Vienna and other Austrian cities; after all, Hitler was born in the small city of Braunau in that country. His demands for the unification of all Germans were then extended to the Sudetenland of Czechoslovakia. He considered it an insult that any Germans should be ruled over by "lowly Slav peasants" and he seemed to have a particular hatred for the Czechs.

Although the German Social Democrats pressed for greater autonomy within Czechoslovakia they were even more anxious to prevent the Nazi takeover of their country. In September 1938, German armies entered unopposed and occupied the Sudetenland by an agreement reached among Britain, France, Italy and Germany–the infamous Munich Agreement. The following year, only one year after the *Anschluss*, Hitler moved into the rest of Czechoslovakia making it the "Protectorate of Bohemia and Moravia." Six months after that tragic event when Germany attacked Poland, Britain and France finally declared war on

Germany, a war that devastated and changed the face of Europe.

In his excellent history of Bohemia, *The Coasts of Bohemia*, Derek Sayers writes, "Czechoslovakia did not suffer as much as many other European countries during the Second World War, if we measure suffering by deaths or material destruction alone. Prague and other Czech cities were relatively unscathed by bombing. Some 360,000 Czech and Slovak nationals perished in the war. Of these–it is immediately necessary to add, since communist sources mostly do not–perhaps 260,000 were men, women and children killed for no other reason than that they were Jewish. The single largest slaughter of Czech citizens in modern history took place far from Bohemia on 8 March 1944, when 3,792 inmates of the 'family camp' at Auschwitz-Birkenau, almost all of the Czech Jews, were gassed in a single night. Reportedly they went to their deaths singing *"Kde domuv Můj,"* the Czech national anthem."

In 1945, Germany was defeated, its former territory divided. Countries such as Poland and Czechoslovakia were liberated and Germans from all over Europe fled or were driven *Heim ins Reich* (Home to the Empire). Czechoslovakia solved its German problem by expelling three million Sudetens. This ethnic cleansing was approved by the four allied powers meeting at Potsdam in July of 1945.

The Skoutajan family originated in Moravia, moved to Vienna in the nineteenth century and later to Bohemia. They were among those who lost their homeland at the end of the Second World War. As I enjoyed my cup of Viennese coffee with Helene I had a sense of having completed a round trip. She told me of the difficult times they experienced after the war when Vienna was an occupied city. The central part of the city was controlled on a rotating basis by the Russian and Western powers. This difficult arrangement had ended only a year before my visit. Vienna was now breathing easier. Once more there was music in the air or did it just feel that way to one "come home"?

CHAPTER FIVE

Genesis

The author's graduation, 1956
B.D., Queen's University

Genesis

What does the Lord require of you,
but to do justice, and to love kindness,
and to walk humbly with your God.
Mica, 6:8

It was the day before Pentecost (1993) and over five hundred people had gathered in the arena at Orangeville, Ontario for the annual meeting of the Toronto Conference of the United Church of Canada. It is a time when all sorts of business is conducted, some of it exciting, much of it less so. Among the events that took place that Saturday morning was the honouring of the retiring ministers. For me, watching those old timers march out for their final hour of glory had never been the most stimulating item on the agenda of the Conference. I was always more energized by debate on resolutions about social justice and world outreach. However, on that occasion retirement had a more subjective tone, it was after all my own.

Along with a dozen others and their spouses decorated with corsages, I was paraded to the platform to be welcomed, thanked and presented with a scroll that declared that I had fought the good fight, had finished the course and was about to draw a pension.

I was one of those chosen to address the assembly that

morning. In my remarks I recalled that a few days earlier I had visited the bookstore at the Church House in Toronto to browse among the latest theological texts. Out of the corner of my eye I noticed a couple dashing around very purposefully. They already had quite a pile of books in their arms and others stacked on the counter which the clerk was tallying up. There were study books, song books and a variety of other useful material, not the sort of literature that I was perusing. With a real sense of excitement in their voices they explained to me and to others within earshot that they had just completed their theological studies and would be ordained within a few days and then go off to a church appointment in northern Alberta. They would be far from an adequate religious bookstore and so were loading up for the long haul.

As we chatted I became aware how distanced I was from their stage of life. Some thirty-seven years separated me from my ordination. I tried to remember that time and immediately sensed all the changes that had occurred during my years of ministry.

I was ordained in 1956 at a time when the world was divided. The Iron Curtain was very real, I had had some personal experience with it. I had crossed the Berlin Wall on a number of occasions to visit with congregations in communist East Germany. Now, that once formidable concrete barrier with its searchlight, guard towers and machine guns that had divided the German people no longer exists. The entire "Eastern Block" that had been held together by the power of the Kremlin was liberated and the Soviet Union itself was splintered into several autonomous republics.

In my address to Conference I remarked that the special guests from the churches in China who had been welcomed earlier were a sign of a new world. A few years ago their visit would not have been possible.

A technological revolution had also taken over the churches that we had served. I doubt that any would be without a computer and I mused whether there had been life before photocopiers. "Remember the old Gestetners with those inky stencils that ruined many a white shirt–gone the way of the dodo."

The year that I was ordained the United Church opened one new church building every week as suburbs sprang up from coast to coast. The 1950s saw a phenomenal upsurge in church membership. But the Barrie tornado that in 1986 had passed within a kilometre of the venue of the annual conference I was chairing (one of my chief claims to fame in the United Church), was not the only storm the church had experienced over the years.

"Indeed, the church has experienced much turmoil," I reminded them. "In the early 1960s it was the introduction of the New Curriculum (a rather theologically radical course of study) that had convulsed the church. Then in the 1980s, it was the ordination of homosexuals that rocked every corner of the church. More recently the restructuring of the church is creating heavy seas. Tomorrow is Pentecost and we will all recall that the church was born in a storm, in the midst of a mighty rushing wind. There is no doubt there will be many storms in the days to come. It has been a great privilege to be part of the crew of this ship. And the ship sails on!"

In the months and years following this event I have done a good deal of thinking about my faith, what inspired it and how I expressed it. I came, after all, out of a non-religious background. My parents in their youth had left their respective churches. Father had been confirmed in the Lutheran Church and mother in the Roman Catholic. Although they had left the institutional church and declared themselves to be "free thinkers," they did not join the organization which bears that name. Among the people we knew it was quite popular at that time. The old Austro-Hungarian empire was too deeply involved with Christendom and "Christianity" had become tainted by political conservatism. There were exciting new winds of change and to some like my parents the social and human values that ought to have been espoused by the church had found a new expression in social democracy. This became their ideological home and they were deeply involved in working for a just and compassionate society. Even as a small child, the table talk I overheard in our home had to do with human rights and political issues. We did not say a table grace but a passion for social justice graced our table.

My father thought and spoke in broad philosophical terms while mother was always more practical and individualistic. There were times when their views clashed. On one such occasion a rather heated debate that turned into a shouting match, mostly on the part of my mother, took place. It terminated with mother angrily abandoning the table, slamming the kitchen door leaving father and me sitting by ourselves looking at our half-eaten meals. He had made the point that the German people as a whole needed to accept some significant responsibility for the rise of fascism. He argued from an historical perspective while mother saw the individual, the captivity of persons in a system, their helplessness against the forces of the time. She stood up for the individual although she was as strong in her condemnation of fascism as my father.

In spite of their political involvement and abandonment of the institutional church, they were a very spiritual people, albeit in a non-traditional sense. They honoured the human spirit. I sensed there was something very deep and powerful that motivated my parents. After coming to Canada they made their spiritual home in the United Church. They appreciated the prophetic witness of people like James Mutchmore and Clarke MacDonald. My father became involved in the organization of the congregation as well as in Presbytery, Conference and General Council. He was especially active in the laymen's movement within the denomination. His liberal views often raised eyebrows in meetings, nevertheless people respected him. "When Felix spoke, we listened," one of the ministers in the Bay of Quinte Conference told me after my father had died.

Mother, on the other hand, played the piano for services in the recreation hall and later the organ at the church we all helped to build in Batawa, near Trenton in eastern Ontario where we lived during and after the war. She baked pies for the Women's Auxiliary and made things for the bazaar. She was excellent in needlecraft. I could tell by her very posture in church that she was somewhat pietistic, but let no one doubt that she was as politically radical as my father. In her youth, my mother had been an active member of a young socialist women's organization. This movement was in fact forbidden in the Austro-Hungarian state. Upon news of her death at age ninety-four, a picture of her appeared in a German newspaper where she is surrounded by young people. The caption hailed her as one who found a way to bring women into politics.

I was born in Aussig, an industrial city in northern Bohemia. As a child I attended a kind of atheist Sunday school where I learned about evolution. Our teacher described primitive society and drew pictures of early cave dwellers and their civilization. I recall how much I enjoyed these sessions. His teaching was far more fascinating than most of the Christian Sunday schools I later experienced.

It was out of this background that I found my way into the church and its ministry. Perhaps in these words I am doing no more than lifting up incidents and experiences so that I might look at them and think about them and discover something about myself. Also I hope to reveal the spirit of the people among whom I grew up. Let me turn to an incident that imprinted itself upon my mind which took place when I was about seven years old.

It was a warm spring evening. My mother and I were among a crowd of several thousand people gathered on the grassy hillside that sloped down to the municipal swimming pool in Aussig [in Czechoslovakia]. The pool was very large and filled with water from a thermal well that kept it at a comfortable temperature. There were in fact four pools, three smaller ones for children and the large pool for adults which was dominated by a very big concrete diving tower with springboards at a variety of levels. Our community was justly proud of this recreational facility. It was a symbol of the care that the community took for all its people. Admission was small and the dressing rooms and canteen were immaculately clean. No one would ever have thought of discarding waste in anything but the refuse baskets. All of us regarded the pool and surrounding park as our own, and so it was.

The rally that evening was not a unique event. The social democratic movement in our city was very strong. Ours was a working class community of about sixty thousand, an industrial centre for coal mining and chemical plants and an important railway junction point. The air in Aussig, as well as the water of the Elbe River, was polluted. The brown coal basin that stretched some forty kilometres west produced smoke and coal dust that set every visitor coughing. The city lay at the confluence of two river valleys, the Elbe which flowed out of the heart of the country northward to Germany and the Bíla from the southwest which drained the industrial basin. Labour unions were very strong in our area and this was an event sponsored by the unions and the Social Democratic Party. May Day was for all of us an important celebration; indeed, it was a national holiday.

Although Aussig was virtually a German city, its people

had a strong sense of being part of the Czechoslovak Republic. We were democratic socialists, not communists, a distinction that was not lost on children even of my own age. I belonged to the Falcons, an organization for children that stressed the solidarity of working class families. We spent much time hiking in the wonderful hill country that surrounded us. We sang songs at campfires and when we marched, we were unashamedly ideological. Our leaders taught us to care for the environment. We were taught that pollution, of which we had plenty of evidence, was one of the hallmarks of capitalist exploitation. Physical fitness programmes in which we were all involved gave us a sense of the value of our bodies. I also belonged to a children's choir. One evening at rehearsal some of us became a bit rowdy, so much so that the conductor slammed the piano lid shut and left abruptly. The organizer of the choir came storming in and scolded us, telling us we were a disgrace to the working class. He made his point after which our director returned and we sang like, pardon me, angels.

I had some difficulty in the youth movement because I did not in fact come from a working class home. My parents were politically active but were thought to be intellectuals although they had not attended university. Indeed, that evening at the pool my father was not sitting with mother and me because as usual he was one of the organizers of the event. I was accustomed to seeing my father address large rallies such as this, but that night the main speaker was the past leader of the Sudeten German social democratic faction in the Czechoslovak government in Prague. Although he was a German his name was Ludvig Czech. He had a powerful presence. He knew how to speak to people and inspire idealistic fervour. He had charisma.

After a variety of presentations by the Atus gymnastic club to which most able bodied socialists belonged, forming pyramids and living statues around the pool, Czech

49

addressed the assembled crowd. He spoke about the place of German social democrats in the Czechoslovak Republic, the international solidarity of working people and the threat of fascism from beyond the borders and from within. Between the frequent rounds of applause, the gathering listened intently.

It was dark as the meeting drew to its conclusion. All lights were out. Although we were several thousand strong one might have heard a pin drop in the grass. Then two searchlight beams swung over the pool and met at the top of the diving tower illuminating a large plain red flag, the international symbol of social democracy, as it waved gently in the evening breeze. It was pure magic. It seemed as though all of us were joined together, our arteries connected to one heart. Trumpets sounded and we sprang to our feet to sing the triumphal marching song of the social democrats, "Brothers, onward to the sun of freedom, brothers onward to the light." Although the words of the song were not gender inclusive, the movement of which we were a part was very much so. Women and men were equal and that equality was celebrated.

It was truly a spiritual event. By and large the social democrats had shed the dogma of religion yet there was no denying a spiritual presence. I had learned in my youth group that the church over the centuries had been closely linked with the oppressors of the working people and a handmaiden of the new and the old aristocracy, capitalism. More recently theologians such as Peter Berger in his Noise of Solemn Assemblies and Doug Hall, a well known professor at McGill University, have made reference to the captivity of the church that took place when the Emperor Constantine accepted Christianity about the year 300 A.D. In his visits to the church in what was then East Germany, Hall found that being a church in disfavour with the state gave them a new freedom. I also felt that in my visits behind the Wall, the church was small but spiritually muscular. However, my first sense of the spiritual was in that May Day celebration.

Although I became a Christian, a minister and a church leader, I have always remembered the power, solidarity and idealism that I first experienced in that movement as a pre-teenager. When I wonder what it was that brought me into the church, I tend to think that Christ had something to do with that movement. Although the church has had a checkered history and has been involved in oppression, even here in Canada, the spirit of its founder influenced other movements even though they never used his name.

The social democratic movement was not the only political force among the Sudetens. Feeding on pan-German nationalism was the Sudeten German Party or Henlein Party as it was commonly known. It was named after its leader Konrad Henlein, a gymnastic instructor who came under the influence of Adolf Hitler in the neighbouring German Reich. This political movement was picking up strength although opposed by the communists and the social democrats. In 1937 the decibel level of the Nazis was growing even in our community. The world around us might have been oblivious to fascism, to concentration camps and anti-Semitism in Germany, but we who lived less than half an hour from the German border were well aware of that lurking evil. There were times when refugees from Germany came to our home and I overheard their conversations with my parents and became familiar with the designation KZ, *Konzentrazions Lager* (concentration camps). Also we had relatives in nearby Dresden who, on their annual Christmas visits, told us about some of the disconcerting things that were going on.

In the winter of 1938 my parents and I went skiing in the hills near the German border. It was wonderful terrain for downhill and cross country skiing. We were making our way up the hills on foot when suddenly, as we came around a curve in the road, we were confronted by Czech soldiers who were building a road block with large logs. We were not allowed to go beyond this point. It was part of the chain of fortifications under construction that would be Czechoslovakia's defence against Germany's army. I was intrigued and not a little worried by what I saw. It was my first experience of the danger that was encroaching upon us. From then on the signs proliferated. For those of us who were born after the First World War and were enjoying as peaceful childhood as I was, a dramatic change was indicated. I was indeed one of the more fortunate victims of the tragedy that followed.

CHAPTER SIX

The Munich Tragedy

Aussig before the Munich Tragedy

The Munich Tragedy

> The Sudetenland is the last territorial claim
> I have to make in Europe.
> *Adolf Hitler: 26 September 1938*

On 13 March 1938, about the time that my family was celebrating my ninth birthday, Hitler marched triumphantly into Austria, the land of his birth. We gathered around the radio and heard the inflammatory speeches of the chancellor as he demanded bringing all German people together in one state. Did that mean us as well? He denounced the oppression and humiliation suffered by Germans at the hands of "lesser" folk. He had an inordinate hatred for the Czechs. From that time on his rhetoric also intensified in the Sudetenland. The German social democrats still maintained a strong position among the electorate but pressure from the Henlein party increased. Their call for *Heim ins Reich* (Home into the empire) intensified among the Sudeten Germans. My home town where Czechs and Germans coexisted in harmony began to take on a new and worrisome nature as Nazis took to the streets in demonstrations and parades.

We had heard rumours about the possibility of a large rally of Nazis in our part of the city. Mother and I were home alone. We spent the supper hour at the living room window looking up the street to The Star, a place where six streets converged. We observed as a small crowd gathered and then watched as it grew alarmingly larger by the minute. It seemed like thousands came together waving swastika flags and shouting fascist slogans. Then, as if by command, the crowd began to move down the street toward our apartment house. We backed away from the window as we heard the crash of glass at the police station across from our home. Word had been passed that all supporters were to have candles in their windows. Of course we refused and were thus marked for attack. But the demonstration moved past our place. Luckily we were located on the third floor and thus overlooked by the surging mob. Beyond our house the Nazis encountered armoured cars of the Czech militia that sent them scattering in all directions. All summer there were such assertions of power but whenever the armoured cars appeared peace seemed to be restored for a few days at least.

The city was taking on a divided nature. As the fascists became more openly aggressive, the social democrats increased their vigilance. The police, however, were not allowed to make arrests although there were skirmishes and thuggery. With support from Germany mounting, the Nazis began to get the upper hand. The Czechs seemed weak; only the Republican Guard, a paramilitary unit of the social democrats, kept order and protected the anti-fascists throughout all of the Sudetenland.

I was returning home for lunch one day in September of 1938, taking my usual shortcut across the football field when suddenly I found myself surrounded by a bunch of boys who had emerged from behind the washrooms. Some of them were wearing the grey shirts and shorts and white socks emblematic of the Henlein youth movement. The attire was in fact forbidden in school, nevertheless they wore it. The school authorities were beginning to weaken in the face of the growing political pressure. The leader of this small gang, whom I recognized, grabbed me and twisted my arm while the others surrounded me. He warned me that if I showed up at school that afternoon I would be beaten up. After pushing me around a bit to give force to their threats, they let me go.

I was terrified and crying when I got home. Father had also come home and I found my parents in a serious discussion. They immediately recognized my terror. When I related my experience they decided that the political situation was getting too hot for comfort. Not only was terrorism on the increase but the proximity of the German border made it likely that Aussig would be a battleground should the German army attack. Rumours of war were abundant; indeed, preparations for evacuation were already in place. We had all been issued gas masks. Oh how I hated them, they were so ugly! A bundle of blankets and clothes was kept ready at all times by the front door.

The decision was made that I would not go back to school but that mother and I would take the train to Prague and beyond to a small hamlet east of the capital in the Czech part of the country where relatives of ours had a farm. I was greatly relieved not to be returning to school and quite excited about going on a trip. We packed up some essentials and then took the streetcar downtown to the railway station. I wondered about my school and what my teacher would think about my absence. There would be at least a couple of boys who would know why I wasn't there. Neither they nor I realized I would never be back.

Father stopped by the bank and withdrew a sizable sum of money before buying our tickets. He saw us off on a train that came from Berlin on its way to Prague. Mother and I found an empty compartment but before the train left we were joined by an acquaintance, a Jewish doctor from our city who was on his way to Prague to attend a meeting. As the train headed up the beautiful Elbe valley I overheard the conversation between mother and our doctor friend. At one point he reached into his vest pocket and brought out a small vial of little white pills. "This is my escape," he said, "if they should catch me." I wondered about his words.

It was dark by the time we reached Prague. Mother had relatives in the city who lived not far from the castle which is quite a long walk from Masaryk Station. We made our way on foot, with mother lugging a suitcase while I carried a backpack. The streets were not unfamiliar, I had often been to this city. We passed the famous Powder Tower, the Old City Square and the astrological clock. From time to time, we paused to rest. I was getting a bit hungry and so we stopped at a place where we bought a sausage and a bun but I could see that mother was anxious to get going again. We crossed the ancient Charles Bridge over the Moldau River and then started the long climb up the steps that led to the castle. Mother pointed out to me the residence of the president. All lights were burning, decisions were being made within that would affect our fate, she told me. At that time Chamberlain of Britain and Daladier of France were negotiating with Hitler in Bad Godesberg. But as it turned out the Czech government was not to be the final arbiter of its own fate.

We found our relatives almost miraculously. Not quite sure of their address, Mother was relying on her memory to find the place, but it was dark and everything looked strange. We were lost but came upon a small police station and went in to inquire. The one policeman on duty smiled and led us through a corridor and knocked on the door of an apartment. It turned out to be the place we'd been looking for. Uncle Palda was surprised to see us. He had just been listening to the radio reports. It didn't look good, he confided. After a late night snack we spent the night in their small apartment just below the castle walls.

The next morning we continued our journey. Uncle Palda (he wasn't really an uncle) escorted us on our way to Wilson Station. We encountered men digging air raid shelters in the parks. There were other signs of preparations for emergencies such as Red Cross tents and a heavy military presence. The city looked different. At the station while waiting for our train, mother and I as usual spoke German with each other but our conversation was rudely interrupted with the command, "Speak Czech!" Fortunately we knew enough Czech to get by, but we certainly were much quieter in public from then on.

By noon we arrived in the little town of Bystřice. Carrying our rucksack and suitcase we walked to the neighbouring hamlet of Mokra Lhota and the Doležal farm, mother's relatives. Father had sent them a telegram to tell them of our coming and they awaited us with open arms. We were assigned to a tiny garret room and fed a good farm dinner. We immediately made ourselves useful by helping them with the potato harvest. In the evening they built a fire at the edge of the field and roasted some potatoes which we ate with salt and butter, a real peasant meal which we enjoyed. A few days later we were joined by my cousin Gert, his mother and our grandmother who were somehow shoe-horned into our attic. Aussig, they told us, had become a turbulent place.

My cousin and I were enrolled in the school at Bystřice and we walked there every day. Czech children were not too well disposed towards us inasmuch as we were German and on at least one occasion I had to rely on the protection of my older and stronger cousin. It brought home rather forcefully the precarious situation in which we found ourselves, hated by the Czechs for being German and on the run from the Germans because we were anti-fascist and pro-Czech.

On our way to school we passed a main railway line and

observed long trains loaded with tanks and guns heading north toward the German border. Our school class was frequently turned over to an older student to supervise while teachers gathered in the office to listen to news reports on the radio. We didn't learn much in those days.

The Czechs were preparing to fight. Indeed, one morning as we looked out of our garret window we saw men leaving their houses, embracing their wives and mothers and then walking down the road to the municipal office where the enlistment was taking place. Conscription had been announced by the Czech government and all able-bodied men were reporting for military service. The scene was both sad and triumphant. The women and children stood in the doorways of their homes waving and dabbing at their eyes. I recall one man gesturing to his wife who stood with tears. "I'll bring you Hitler's head!" he shouted. The small nation seemed ready to defend itself against the German bully.

Father had remained in Aussig where the Republican Guard (RW) was maintaining some semblance of order. The *Volkshaus*, not far from my father's office, was the headquarters of the Social Democratic Party. On the top floor were offices, then meeting rooms and on the ground floor a restaurant where, over beer, plans were discussed and gossip exchanged. My father spent a good deal of time there meeting with his colleagues. One day the Henleins made an attempt to raid the building but the RW was prepared. They allowed the gang to reach the top floor but when they got there the RWs overwhelmed them and pitched them down the stairs. At each landing more RWs were now waiting to propel them downward until they landed on the street. There was great celebration that night; refreshments flowed freely at the Volkshaus beerstube. It was, however, only a temporary triumph. The Nazis were going to have their revenge.

One day my father got a phone call at his office from the police chief, who was a Czech, inviting him and his colleague to come to his office. They were courteously received. The chief and his two guests had a pleasant but rather inconsequential conversation, so much so that they began to suspect other motives for the invitation. Presently the chief reached into his drawer and brought out a file which he opened on his desk. He then got up and excused himself and left the office. My father and his friend looked at each other questioningly, then my father got up and moved around the desk to see what the file was all about. He discovered that it was a document from a Nazi cell that the police must have raided. It contained the names of all the people who were to be rounded up and taken to Dachau (the infamous concentration camp near Munich where many Sudeten anti-fascists suffered during the war) immediately after the Nazi takeover.

Father and his friend quickly scribbled down the names which included his own and then took their seats again. Shortly thereafter the chief returned, sat down behind his desk, closed the file and returned it to the drawer. He then rose to his feet, extended his hand to them, thanked them for coming and wished them good health. They departed in the knowledge that the chief had afforded them the privilege of seeing their own warrant of arrest.

Time was running out. Hitler was having his way with Chamberlain and Daladier. They were trying to be conciliatory. Lord Runciman of Britain had been to Czechoslovakia to study the situation and report back to the British Foreign Office. From the very outset, Runciman was in favour of a partition of the country but his research was rather one-sided. It is reported that he only met with the wealthy who were pro-German. When confronted with a petition from the Social Democrats, Runciman ignored them and their statement. Thus when he returned home, he advocated the dismemberment of the country.

When father returned to the Volkshaus, he found tensions were very high indeed. He shared the list of names with the others. In the meantime, reports were constantly coming in from other parts of the country. Henlein raids were becoming ever more daring and vicious. The Czech police seemed unable to put them down. There were all kinds of rumours circulating; some reported that fighting had broken out, that the German Army had been repulsed, that the Russians were coming to the aid of Czechoslovakia and were taking up positions. Most of these proved false, mere wishful thinking. The RW realized they were alone fighting a losing battle but were nevertheless determined to continue to the bitter end.

The air was thick with cigarette smoke. Everyone was clustered around the radio which was bringing news updates from Prague and Munich. And then it was all over. The so-called Allies, Britain and France, had succumbed to the demands of Hitler. The Czech delegation was not included in the discussions, instead a fait accompli was handed to them. Chamberlain had returned to Britain announcing the infamous "peace in our time" and the German armies began their incursion over the mountains into the Sudetenland of Czechoslovakia unopposed.

It is indeed sad to read the account of those September days as Hitler postured and threatened to get his way. It is embarrassing to remember the weak-kneed response of the Allies. It is devastating to note that the German military staff at the highest level was planning a coup d'etat against Hitler if he forced a military confrontation with what they believed was a powerful Czech army in highly fortified terrain, especially if there was any possibility that France and Britain would be drawn into the conflict. One cannot help but wonder what might have happened, how many lives might have been saved. The Jewish Holocaust might have been averted. Perhaps the world could have spared itself the Cold War, if only Chamberlain and Daladier had been more courageous. It has been suggested that the Allied leaders were more concerned about communism; indeed, Bonnet, the French foreign minister, is quoted to have said that Germany could be employed in a common front against communist Russia. There was at that time a good deal of sympathy for Hitler even at the highest levels of the British government. The British foreign office had instructed the members of their Olympic team to give the Hitler salute when attending the 1936 Olympic games in Berlin. As late as that summer of 1938, Canadian Prime Minister Mackenzie King had pronounced Herr Hitler "an honourable man." King, a believer in extrasensory perception, did not have a very clear message from beyond. One voice rang out in Britain, that of Winston Churchill, who warned parliament of Hitler's plans. Churchill was, however, denounced as an irresponsible war-monger. His warning, of course, proved to be prophetic.

As I reread the accounts of those days I find myself getting excited as if reading an historic novel. Hope builds up inside me, although I am conscious of the outcome, that somehow the course of history could be different. I discover sweat on my palms holding the book as I read of the plans to topple Hitler reaching to almost minutes before its accomplishment. But then suddenly the Allies' acquiescence takes the wind out of the sails of the plotters. Hitler got all and more than he imagined would be granted and without a shot being fired. He did a little victory dance we are told. Czechoslovakia now stood nude and defenseless before the enemy.

The Munich Agreement and Chamberlain's "Peace" are famous but little is known of the consequences as they affected the people of that area immediately and after the war had ended.

In my father's correspondence I discovered a letter from his friend written after the war, which recalls that last night in Aussig. It is an account shrouded in despair not only for their own lives but for the country and for the ideology for which they had been prepared to give their lives. They had met at the Volkshaus to talk over their fate and after a couple of beers they shook hands and wished each other farewell. Father headed for the station accompanied by two RW guards to catch the last train for Prague.

The following afternoon while our hosts were thrashing, my father suddenly appeared at the farm gate. It was a hot day and the yard was in turmoil, straw flying everywhere. My cousin and I were busy gathering it up. As I looked up, sweat blurring my eyes, I saw him standing at the gate. He opened it and slowly came towards me, looking tired, unshaven and defeated. Mother also saw him and we rushed over. We fell into each other's arms and, for the first time in my life, I saw tears streaming down his cheeks. He was virtually speechless except, "Everything is lost," I heard him say.

CHAPTER SEVEN

Refugees

Wenzel Jaksch,
Leader of the Sudeten Social Democrats

Refugees

The German dictator, instead of snatching the victuals
from the table, has been content to have them
served to him course by course.
Winston Churchill in House of Common, 5 October, 1938

On 1 October 1938, German troops marched, or rather drove, into the Sudetenland. This was a new kind of army that was prepared to fight on wheels rather than from trenches or fixed positions. They had perfected the technology of the Blitzkrieg–they moved with lightning speed before the enemy could be ready. Nevertheless, when the generals and even Hitler himself saw the fortifications the Czechs had built in the mountains they had grave doubts about their ability to overcome them without serious losses. As in Aussig so also in most of the Sudetenland, huge crowds of Nazi supporters joyfully awaited the troops. The city was decorated with flags and red, white and black bunting. Pictures of Hitler, Goebels and Goering appeared in the windows of homes and storefronts. The populace seemed to be well prepared for this event. At the same time, however, anti-fascists were fleeing by the thousands.

What now? This was the question our family group in Mokra Lhota had to contemplate. There were rumours that all would be forgiven, that no one would face incarceration in the concentration camps; however, we were skeptical. One thing was sure: there would be no war, at least not right away. My uncle, who was a locomotive engineer, had remained behind and indeed was able to continue in his job. His skill was very much needed by the new German administration. Next morning my cousin, my aunt and grandmother decided to return to Aussig encouraging us to join them.

In Czechoslovakia all nonresidents of a community had to register at the local police station and so my father went to the precinct office in Bystřice nearby. He was questioned and then told that because we were German we would not be able to remain with our relatives in Mokra Lhota beyond forty-eight hours. Thus we had to move. Since returning to Aussig was out of the question for Father, our hope was that we could find accommodation in Prague where many refugees were gathering. It was also to Prague that the leadership of the Sudeten Social Democrats had moved. We gathered our few belongings, said goodbye to our relatives who had been so kind to us and took the train to the capital.

Adorned by hundreds of church spires and dominated by the Hradčany castle, Prague is a beautiful city. It was a cosmopolitan community, being home to Germans and Czechs and a large Jewish population. Although Vienna had been the capital of the Austro-Hungarian empire, Prague was a close rival especially in the realm of culture. For a time in the fourteenth century it was the seat of Charles IV of the Holy Roman Empire. He had spent much money and effort to make Prague a true capital. He established a university, built the castle and the well known Charles bridge that leads across the Moldau River to the hill on which the castle and cathedral are located. At that time, Prague was virtually a German city.

Seven hundred years ago German settlers moved into

Bohemia and Moravia. As long ago as the twelfth to the fourteenth century, Germans were encouraged to migrate to this largely rural area. Skilled craftsmen were required to work the silver mines. Administrators and business entrepreneurs were needed for new urban developments. These Germans soon constituted a new middle class and their language became the language not only of commerce but also of the intelligentsia. For centuries Germans and Czechs lived together in this area in relative peace although Czechs and their language suffered from an inferiority complex which continued into the nineteenth century. However, over the latter half of that century there was an awakening among the Czechs and Moravians. A new consciousness of their culture and history was fostered. The Czechs began to long for independence from their Austro-German overlords. There had been a time when the Czech language was regarded as no more than a kind of peasant patois. To rise above one's state, fluency in German was required. Then a national awakening took place. Writers, musicians, composers and philosophers pushed for the acceptance of Czech as a "real" language of a "real" people. This inevitably led to a movement for political independence. Thus at the end of the First World War, Bohemia, Moravia and Slovakia were severed from Austria. Czech became the language of the new state but accommodation was made for the large ethnic communities in the country including the three and a half million Germans as well as the Magyars and Poles.

It was difficult for the Germans in this new country, who had always considered themselves as an elite, to feel that now in spite of such accommodations as German schools and municipal administrations, they were no longer "in charge." Czechs also took advantage of their new power. The tables were turned; advancement not only in the public but also in the private sphere demanded bilingualism. Even then there were countless incidents when Czechs were

69

given preferential treatment. A case in point: although my uncle Max spoke Czech fluently, he was unable to move from the position of fireman to engineer on the locomotives until after the German takeover. Without a doubt, this situation chafed and led to ethnic unrest and a demand for rights and powers.

Germans and other minorities had hoped that the modern Czechoslovakia would adopt something of the cantonal system of Switzerland but most Czechs were negative toward such an accommodation. This was now their country and it was Czech; even Slovaks, ethnic cousins if not siblings, felt offended. In the meantime Germany was struggling back from the defeat of the First World War and the degradation foisted upon the Germans by the Treaty of Versailles. Although humbled, they maintained a sense of pride and determination to reassert themselves as a continental power. The political situation was ideal for the arrival of a demagogue who would play on their national aspirations.

Undoubtedly Germans in Czechoslovakia saw what was happening across the mountains with a variety of feelings. To some it gave a sense of Germanness and an enhanced desire to belong to this nation rather than be part of an ethnic minority. But there were also those who feared what they saw happening–the anti-Semitism, the intolerance of anything not German and above all an anti-labour conservatism. Democratic socialism was, for a large number of the Germans especially those who worked in industry, the political philosophy of choice. They thus developed a powerful political movement in which my parents played an important role. They had no appetite for an independent state, they simply wanted a greater autonomy in the regions where they were dominant, especially the highly industrial Sudetenland. The Swiss cantonal system would have been my parents' first choice for political structure. Their leaders, Ludwig Czech, a member of parliament in Prague and his successor Wenzel Jaksch, fought hard to achieve that goal. Social democrats regarded with suspicion and at times outright animosity the political movement on their left, the Communist Party with its sponsor in not-so-distant Russia.

However, slow progress and obvious resistance on the part of the Czech government led many Germans to the side of the Henlein movement which promised nothing less than *Heim ins Reich*. I recall one of my childhood friends whose parents were members of that party describing to me how *Heim ins Reich* would take place. Trucks would come, he explained, and all the Germans would be loaded and taken north across the mountains to the Reich. He proved to be prophetic although this was not quite the way Konrad Henlein had envisioned it.

In the first week of October our small family arrived back in Prague. The beautiful baroque city was now crowded with refugees. The wealthier ones had taken most of the hotel accommodation while the rest were put up in makeshift refugee quarters within the city as well as in the countryside. The Czech police were actively turning back those seeking asylum; indeed, whole train loads of fleeing people ended up in the waiting arms of the SS and Gestapo. In the postwar letter from my father's friend previously cited, he tells of being interrogated time and again and always it seemed they were trying to determine my father's whereabouts. Over thirty thousand Sudetens were sent to concentration camps from which many did not return.

Since Father had many friends and was well known in the movement, we were able to find accommodation at the Union Hotel. The Monopol Hotel on Hibernska street now took over the role of the *Volkshaus*. It was a familiar place for me. It was also a likely place to find us and so a few days later my grandmother once more appeared on the scene. Ever the mother hen trying to bring her brood together, she persuaded her daughter to return to Aussig. Mother made the decision that she would test the water, a very foolish decision as it would turn out to be. In retrospect I have come to the conclusion that under the pressures of the time, our family came very close to dissolution. My parents protected me and I was oblivious to the tensions that existed between them. Or was I? Deep within me there were fears and I felt torn. I was totally committed to my mother and loved and respected my father.

On the morning of 25 October, Mother and I said goodbye to Father and boarded a bus to Aussig. Crossing the provisional boundary between the Sudetenland and what remained of Czechoslovakia proved to be no problem. By noon we had arrived in our home town.

The city was transformed, so much so that I scarcely recognized it as home. The Nazi flags, so alien to me, bedecked the streets and the hated pictures of Hitler and his henchmen adorned all store windows. *"Heil Hitler!"* was the expected greeting that I found hard to get my tongue around, yet to abstain would immediately rouse suspicions of political dissidence. I still find it hard to countenance that I had used that greeting, it haunts me like a bad dream. Police now wore unfamiliar uniforms and, of course, there were many soldiers on the streets.

My mother's brother, Dolf, a confectioner, met us at the bus station. It was a tense reunion. "You will come and stay with us," he insisted, and then whispered that our apartment was under surveillance. Fears and suspicions were raised and we began to wonder whether indeed we had made a grave mistake. When we finally did venture to our former home we found that the door was sealed by the police as a protection against vandalism, or so it was said. The German authorities were somewhat surprised how easily the Sudetenland had fallen into their hands and were quite unprepared to take over control so quickly.

Consequently our arrival back was not noticed immediately although perhaps they hoped that if nothing untoward happened to us, Father might be enticed to return.

We decided to move from our apartment where I had lived all nine years of my life. I knew no other home. We found a smaller place closer to where my uncle lived and made it look as though our return was permanent. I was even registered in a new school although I never attended. Only when friends attempted to move our furniture to our new location was our presence noted. They had broken the seal and were confronted by the police and explained to them that we were back and moving to another residence. "Well then we shall soon meet them," the police said but did not stop them from their task. The furniture was moved to our new home but I felt quite unhappy and a stranger there. Also, I missed my father very much.

One evening shortly after our move just as I was falling asleep, I vaguely heard a knock on our door. Mother answered and there were some moments of quiet discussion. I was wakened early next morning while it was still dark and told to pack my rucksack with some clothes and one favourite toy. There was no doubt what that would be, my electric train, one of the first miniature trains made that I had received the previous Christmas. I wrapped it in my clothes and stashed it in my backpack. My uncle arrived and we quietly slipped away. The "underground" had found out that we would be "picked up" soon; also, they had a message from my father in Prague informing us of the possibility that we might escape to Britain.

The streets were shrouded in fog as Mother and I walked to the station. My uncle walked ahead of us almost out of sight. At the station he purchased our tickets while we waited outside. Only when the train pulled into the station did we come onto the platform. We quickly boarded, but now we faced a new dilemma. In order to reach Prague we would have to cross the new border which every day was getting more difficult. We had no passport or indeed any documents. Mother decided on the excuse that we were returning to Prague to pick up our possessions; indeed, we held return tickets, but we knew that this was not enough. She decided that we should leave the train at Lovosice, the last stop before the border, in order to explain to someone our mission and obtain a temporary pass. We were not alone in our compartment in the train, a woman Mother knew was also there. She too was travelling to Prague but had a passport and exit permission. Mother took a risk and confided in her and asked her to contact Father when she got to Prague.

The train stopped at Lovosice and Mother and I went to the waiting room. "Sit by our baggage and don't talk to anyone, wait until I return. Don't be afraid, it might take quite awhile." With that she left the station. I am not sure how long she was gone–it seemed many hours. People came and went but no one approached me. Anxiety can make time seem long or short, but I was confident that Mother would return. I watched the door like a hawk. Finally, I believe it was three hours later, she reappeared. In her hand she clutched some official looking papers. She seemed tense but very efficient. "Get our stuff," she ordered. A taxi waited by the curb. We climbed into the back seat together and off we went, Mother tightly clasping my hand.

On the train my mother's mind had been racing to find a solution for our dilemma. Then it occurred to her that she had relatives in Leitmeritz, a neighbouring city, who operated the restaurant at city hall. Mother also knew they were Nazi sympathizers. After leaving me at the station, she had taken a bus to visit the relatives. She told them of her intention to return to Prague to retrieve our bedding and her need of a temporary pass. As proof she showed them our return tickets. What was needed from them was an affidavit, an *Unbedenklichkeitszeugnis*. This they readily provided and with it in hand she went to the authorities located in the city hall just upstairs from the restaurant. A temporary border crossing certificate was issued to Gertrude Skoutajan on 3 November 1938 as shown on page 76. Her "uncle" went with her and smoothed the way to obtaining the pass to Prague. Did this "uncle" know? Was blood stronger than ideology?

We tried to look composed as our taxi approached the border. Two large hay wagons had been pulled across the road so traffic would have to wind its way around them. Our car stopped. A guard came to our window and Mother surrendered her papers. He looked them over, looked at us, spoke briefly to the driver and then waved us through the narrow space between the wagons. It was as simple as that. We were now in no man's land between the Czech and German borders. At the next check point a kilometre down the road Mother again presented her papers, this time to a Czech guard. I was relieved to see a familiar uniform once again though I must admit that the German uniforms were far more spiffy. Mother gave her alibi in Czech. The guard then inspected the car and discovered the driver had tarred over the Czech on the license plates. He ordered the driver to scrape it clean, which he did with reluctance. Meanwhile Mother and I sat in silence. When the driver had completed his job to the guard's satisfaction our papers were returned and we were allowed to proceed.

Our destination was Theresienstadt, now Terezín, the location of the infamous prison where Jews and political prisoners were later housed and from which the Jews were transported to slave labour camps or crematoria in Auschwitz or Buchenwald. Even during the Austrian time, Terezín had served as a military prison. We drove past its ugly walls on our way to the town square where a bus was loading for Prague. Mother arranged with our taxi driver to

Paſſierſchein

zum Überſchreiten der deutſchen Sicherungslinie.

Der
Die _Gertrud Skoutajan_ (Vorname) (Zuname) geb. am _14. 1. 1901_

in _Auſſig_ wohnhaft in _Auſſig_ (Ort und Straße)

iſt berechtigt, die deutſche Sicherungslinie von Lobofit, nach

Bauſchowitz und zurück bei _Hirſchowitz_ (Ort der Überſchreitung)

zu überſchreiten.

Dieſer Ausweis iſt ohne Aufforderung den deutſchen Poſten vorzuzeigen. Über=
ſchreiten der Sicherungslinie außerhalb der oben bezeichneten Übertrittsſtelle iſt
verboten. Wer dem zuwiderhandelt, begibt ſich in Lebensgefahr. Dieſer Ausweis
iſt nicht übertragbar und gilt vom **3. XI.** 1938 bis _4. 11. 38_

(Ort und Datum)
Dienſtſtempel

(Unterſchrift)
Dienſtgrad und Dienſtſtellung

Verlängerungsvermerk.

Dieſer Ausweis wird vom   bis   verlängert

(Ort und Datum)

(Unterſchrift)
Dienſtgrad und Dienſtſtellung

Dienſtſtempel

Temporary border crossing certificate issued to
Gertrude Skoutajan on 3 November 1938

pick us up in two days' time and paid him in full for both trips for which he gave her a receipt. All this was important to prove to anyone that we were only temporarily in the country. We had heard that refugees were being turned back with dreadful consequences. Mother also bought return tickets from the bus driver. On the bus we spoke Czech together just enough to let the other passengers know that we were not German. The bus was totally filled by the time it left the town square. We felt relieved to be on our way and looked forward to our reunion with Father.

Less than half an hour out of Terezín the bus was stopped by the police. An officer boarded the bus and after looking over the passengers asked the driver whether he was carrying any *ubrchliki* (refugees). The driver said no, after all we had return tickets. The policeman saluted the driver and once more we were off. We could breathe again.

In another hour the bus entered the outskirts of Prague and made its way to Wilson Station. As we rounded the park in front of the large railway station which also served as a bus terminal I caught sight of my father hurrying across the street. I was somewhat shocked to see him wearing a cloth cap, not his hat. It seemed so out of character to me, but oh how happy I was to see him, whatever his headgear. Our friend on the train had managed to contact him at the Monopol Hotel to give him the news that we were on our way. We stumbled off the bus and into each other's arms.

Walking into the Monopol Hotel was like coming home. It was the headquarters of the Sudetens and we immediately saw many familiar faces. Mother was greeted enthusiastically. Everyone wanted to know about our visit to Aussig and what we had experienced there. I was never so glad to be together again. We hadn't eaten all day, not even breakfast, and we were very hungry. The tensions of the day had made us forget about food. We went for dinner and while we ate Father explained the plans for our move to Britain. He had brought me a map of Europe and showed me the roundabout way through Poland we would be going.

Father explained that the Sudeten refugee organization through Wenzel Jaksch had made arrangements with the British government and specifically with the Labour Party to accept two thousand refugees from the Sudetenland. There were evidently some rather tender consciences in Britain over the Munich Agreement. Chamberlain's "Peace in our time" was not universally applauded by those who recognized Hitler's ambitions for what they were. Father also told us that those most endangered would leave first, some by plane but most by train and ship through Poland, the Baltic and North Sea. There were some soft spots in this route. Travelling through Poland was risky inasmuch as Poland and Czechoslovakia did not enjoy the best relations. Indeed, Poland had designs on a small region called Teschen. Britain was not the only destination, some had already gotten out to Sweden and France. One other problem was that Czechoslovakia would have to provide passports to people who now were technically German subjects. Thus "interim" passports were to be issued that the host countries would accept. A great deal of negotiating had

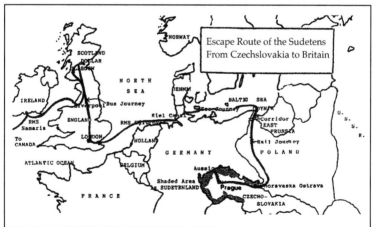

Escape Route of the Sudetens From Czechoslovakia to Britain

gone into these arrangements on the part of Jaksch and others. Unfortunately it looked as though men would be split from their families and we would be in Prague alone for a number of weeks. This did not thrill my mother, indeed, she became quite still and pensive. But for the moment we were together and surrounded by people we knew. My parents even went to the opera that night.

Next morning we moved out of our hotel to the attic of an apartment house not far from Wilson Station. We were to share a large room under the roof of the house with a dozen other refugees. Straw mattresses lay side by side on the floor. We arranged our suitcases to fence off a little area for ourselves. We shared the same fate as these people and quickly got to know each other. It soon seemed as though we were one large family.

I became a bit of an entertainer. As a child I was very flexible of limb and a bit of a contortionist. I accomplished such feats as putting my ankles behind my head and eating sandwiches in that grotesque position much to the amusement of our fellow refugees. I was also able to cross my legs in a peculiar fashion and walk on my knees, which always brought howls of laughter from everyone. I suppose all were longing for anything to take their minds off our uncertain future.

It was now a waiting game. Each day we went to the Workers' Hall, a large establishment of the Prague Labour Council where refugees were given a free meal and a little bit of money to tide us over. Mother had spent quite a bit of our resources on tickets and the taxi driver to ease us across the border. Father did have some money in reserve in a bank in Prague but all this could quickly disappear. We needed clothing, having left almost everything behind. My parents bought me several "American" shirts. They were plaid and very colourful and buttoned all the way up the front unlike the shirts I was accustomed to that had only an opening for the neck. I really loved them and wanted to wear them all the time. Sometimes, for a change, we went to eat at the Bata shoe store cafeteria on the top floor of their store on Wenzeslaus Square. It was a place where one could enjoy good meals at very reasonable prices. Little did we guess that some day in the not so distant future all of us would be working for that company in distant Canada.

We had a lot of time on our hands and while Father spent much of his time with the refugee organization, Mother and I did a lot of sightseeing. I got to know the city well. We visited every museum and gallery and I got to see the insides of almost every church. We also acquired a book of English instruction and spent a lot of time learning vocabulary and expressions.

Mail service had been restored between the Sudetenland and the rest of Czechoslovakia and we were once again in contact with our relatives in Aussig. Of course, they had to be careful what they wrote, sending it to a postal box in Prague. One day Father got a letter from Germany offering him a job with the infamous *Stuermer*, an anti-Semitic newspaper. Father felt insulted but of course saw it to be a ploy to get him to come back. It also made us aware that our whereabouts were known.

A few days after our arrival in Prague the first group of refugees left for Britain. We went to the Masaryk Station to see them off. The group consisted of men only, some of whom we knew quite well. Among them was Haufe, a very active social democrat whom the Nazis would have loved to get their hands on. His young wife, a Viennese woman, stood with us and waved as the train pulled out of the station. Haufe stood on the observation platform of the last car. We all watched until the train disappeared from view and wondered where or whether we would meet again. Britain seemed so far away and there were no guarantees. We dreaded the day when it would be our turn to say goodbye. That day came soon.

Was Mother trying to protect me or herself? We decided not to go to the station to see Father off but say our goodbyes in the attic. She and I then left for the airport to spend the day watching planes take off and land. I had never seen an airplane on the ground and it proved to be a good distraction. In the evening we returned to our attic and straw mattresses. I know Mother wept after I had closed my eyes.

The waiting continued. Each day, Mother visited the refugee offices to enquire about news of our turn to depart the country. Mother and I strolled the streets looking longingly at the warm lights that glowed inside, envying every home. Family was very important to my mother and I knew that she was once again playing with the thought of returning to Aussig. Later she confided to me that she could not countenance people persuading me that my father was a *Sozi Schwein* (a socialist pig). And then there was the possibility that they might imprison us to force Father to return. She confessed to me much later that the thought of jumping from the roof of our building had also crossed her mind, but then what would become of me? And so we passed the days learning English while sitting on the banks of the Moldau River.

Was it a miracle or was it coincidence, or does it really matter? It was a dull November day and we wandered the streets as usual nibbling on our bar of hard chocolate. Breakfast had consisted of a cup of coffee and a bun. We had no particular goal in mind. There was still lots more to see in this historic city. For a time we wandered down the narrow alleys looking into store windows, admiring what they had that we could not buy. We came upon a toy store with electric trains in the show window and I saw one that was much like the one I had brought in my rucksack from home. There were also passenger cars, sleepers and a dining car with lights in it. My longing was obvious and we recalled that last Christmas "at home." My parents could hardly wait until the parlour doors were opened and I would see that much longed for train under the tree. These memories intensified our homesickness and loneliness.

"Where will we be this Christmas?" I should not have asked the question but it was uppermost in my mind. Mother turned her head away so that I would not see the tears welling up in her eyes. She put her arm around me and together we walked along the cobbled street past a group of musicians playing familiar tunes. Mother. who was a music lover, found it hard to pass by without leaving a coin in their hats, but now it seemed that every penny counted. We weren't destitute, at least not yet, but of course we had no idea how long we would have to survive before the situation was resolved, whatever that meant. All was in uncertainty.

Our walk brought us out on the Old Town Square dominated by the giant statue of Jan Hus, the famous Czech reformer who hundreds of years ago was burned at the stake. Now in stone he is remembered as a folk hero by both Catholics and Protestants. Hus had thought he had safe passage in order to defend his radical theological ideas before a court in Germany. Silencing him, however, was more important to his enemies than fulfilling that guarantee. Mother let slip, "Life hasn't changed that much."

Before leaving the square we stood for a few moments before the famous Astrological Clock. The ten o'clock bell began to toll and the figures of the apostles came out the little door and disappeared again on the other side. When it was over the skeleton gave a tug on the rope that sounded a single chime to remind the watchers of their mortality. We hardly needed such a sign.

We had been to this spot at other times–better days. Aussig was not too far away and, on occasion, we had accompanied Father on business trips to Prague. We always planned to be at the clock at noon to watch as the bell tolled twelve times. Memories upon memories, would we also remember these perplexing times?

We crossed the Moldau by the Charles Bridge. Together, hand in hand, we walked across this ancient bridge past the statues of the saints located on every pier. The river looked gray as it slid under the spans. We recalled Smetana's tone poem, "The Moldau," which described this river as it springs in the mountains and then winds its way through the forests and meadows, past villages and towns, tumbles over waterfalls and then flows majestically out to the great North Sea. We recalled a performance of this composition in our wonderful theatre in Aussig. When would we hear the beautiful music again?

I spied some ducks on the river. "Do you suppose," I asked, "if they allowed themselves to be carried by the current they would drift past Aussig?" No one would demand passports or papers from them, I thought. "How long would it take them to get there?" I continued. Mother didn't answer, nor did I expect a reply. I was just talking to myself.

We crossed the river to the Small Side, as it is called, which is dominated by the hill and its castle and the towers of St. Vitus Cathedral behind. Without a definite destination in mind we wandered up the long passage of stairs that followed the castle walls and were reminded of that night when we first left Aussig and searched these very streets for our relatives' home. So much had happened in those few weeks.

From time to time we stopped and turned around to look out over the city. It seemed veiled in mist. We were used to walking; that's all we had done since Father left. Then a hint of rain spurred us on to the cathedral where we could wait out the shower. It was a short distance and soon we entered the great wooden doors leading into the vast interior of the church. The smell of incense greeted us.

Uprooted and Transplanted

Although Mother had abandoned the Catholic faith a long time before, she dipped her finger in the holy water and marked the sign of the cross on her body. I didn't follow her example but nevertheless sensed a presence that I could not understand. No one had to tell me to whisper.

I had been in this church before and had always wanted to go on the guided tours of the crypts under the nave where the ancient kings of Bohemia lie buried. Indeed, it seemed that a group was just lining up at the entrance. Mother produced a coin and I went off to join the tour. I decided to keep my mouth shut and not reveal that I was German. I followed a group of school children and was able to understand what the teacher was telling them. There were also a few adults on the tour who did not belong to the school group. I caught a few words and determined they must be English tourists.

From time to time our procession through the underground passages stopped at some marker. The teacher told about an artist or author who had been buried there. The tourists opened their guide books and tried to read them in the dim light of that place. I was glad I wasn't the last, I had heard of someone being accidentally locked in overnight, a scary prospect.

Our group arrived at the central point of the crypts. Before us was a barred door beyond which was a well lit room. In the centre of it stood the sarcophagi of three Bohemian kings. The children stopped their chatter and we all stood in quiet awe. This was a special place which spoke of a history of which the Czechs were proud indeed. Once they had been a powerful nation. Hitler and his armies would not be able to squelch that spirit.

Again, I sensed that familiar ambivalent feeling. I was German not Czech, but it was the Germans from whom we fled. I decided these school children would not be able to grasp this seeming contradiction. I don't know how long the tour had taken, not quite an hour I had thought. The group now came to a set of stairs that led upward to the nave of the church. As I approached the door, my eyes were blinded by a powerful light. It had been dark down below. As I emerged, I discovered the church was filled with light which was streaming through the colourful stained glass windows. I was awestruck by the transformation. I looked about for Mother but could not locate her. Everything looked different in the bright light. The place where we had sat was empty. But then I heard my name.

"Hannsi," she called, "I'm here." I turned and saw my mother smiling. I immediately noticed there was something different about her. When I had left her she looked depressed and tired, but now she looked like her old self, confident and happy, the way I remembered her in better times.

She took my arm, not like mother and child but more like lovers. We walked toward the great door. Before we left Mother turned briefly and gave a small but meaningful nod toward the altar and then we walked out into the bright sunlight. We went to a sausage stand nearby and ordered up a little lunch. We sat down under a massive chestnut tree. It didn't seem to matter to her that the bench was damp.

Mother seemed anxious to get going again and I finally had to ask, "Where are we going in such a hurry?"

"The secretariat," she said. This was not unusual, we often visited the place where we expected to hear news about our future travel and get letters from Father. Mother had been quite persistent with them. She had known some of the people for quite a long time. And so we set off. The way was downhill this time and we virtually ran down the slippery steps. I was elated, I hadn't seen my mother in this mood for quite a while.

We crossed the Moldau once more but this time the street musicians received a crown. It seemed like no time

85

before we arrived at Wenzeslaus Square and proceeded down a small alley to the old office building that housed the refugee organization. We went to the office of Ernst Paul, an old friend and colleague of my father's we had seen numerous times but always to receive the news that there was no message from Father and no news about our transportation to Britain. This time, however, Paul greeted us with a smile. He handed Mother a letter in familiar handwriting. At last, a letter from Father, postmarked Scotland. She tore it open but before she could begin to read it Paul handed her another larger envelope. It was quite bulky but without a stamp. She put down Father's letter and opened the other. It contained a passport, two railway tickets, a sheet of instructions and a cache of travel money.

Paul said, "Hurry up, get ready. Your transport leaves tomorrow evening from Wilson Station. Be there at six o'clock." Mother didn't quite know what to do first, read the letter or inspect the documents that she had been waiting for almost despairingly. Or should we rush back to the attic to begin our packing, that would take no time at all? She gave Paul a big hug. It would be the last time she would see him. Then together we raced down the stairs.

On the square we found a table in front of a restaurant. With the sun out again, the sidewalk cafe was once more in business. She ordered two cups of coffee and two pieces of Linzer torte and then, while we waited, she tore open the letter from my father. I could see her eyes racing over the pages and then she realized that I ought to be included in this news.

"Dearest Trude and Hannsi," the letter began, "Greetings from Scotland. We arrived here three days ago and are living in a castle. The trip was hard but no harder than leaving you. I think it was the right thing that you did not take Hanns to the station. It was best that we said our goodbyes at the attic." At this point Mother stalled, she remembered the day. She especially remembered returning home to find Father and his suitcase were gone. I knew the other refugees were silently watching us. They brought us chocolate bars and tried to include us in their group.

Mother looked up into the sky and took another swallow of coffee and then continued to read to me. "The trip from Prague to Brno was uneventful. Unfortunately because of some hitch in the timetable we were given we missed our connecting train and had to spend the night at the station waiting hall. Early next morning we caught another train that took us toward Slovakia where we had to cross the Tatra mountains. The territory was beautiful but our minds were concentrated on getting across the border into Poland. That proved to be easier than we had contemplated, however, there were other problems awaiting us, but of that later."

"Nevertheless we arrived in Gdynia in the early hours of the next morning. After waiting for an hour at the station a representative of the steamship company came to meet us. Our luggage was taken by truck but we had to walk through the city to the harbour. We boarded a freighter called the SS *Baltrover* which took us via the Kiel canal to Britain. Our escort, an Englishman, a member of the British parliament who travels back and forth between London and Prague, told us that in the future they would be able to send a railway car straight through from Prague to Gdynia. Hanns would find the walk through the hill country rather demanding. I am hoping for the best. The sea journey was rather rough and most of us got sick on the North Sea. One of our group lost his false teeth overboard."

"We are now in Scotland where it has rained every day since our arrival. We are living in a rather palatial castle and feel like privileged people especially after the hardships of our travels. I am sure that Hanns will find it an interesting place to live. It has a high turret from which you can see much of the surrounding landscape."

"Our thoughts are with our loved ones and I look forward to the day when we shall be together again. May it be real soon and may you have a smooth trip. I embrace you both with all my love."

At this point, Mother could no longer hold herself together. Tears ran down her cheeks and her body shook as she clenched my hand until it hurt. We both could scarcely believe that the journey would happen, but here in our hands was the passport and ticket that seemed to say, yes, it will.

Mother couldn't finish her cake. I did, nibbling away while she was reading. When we arrived at the attic it was completely empty, only our baggage and the straw mats remained. The rest had left. We did not know where they had gone. It was hard to sleep all alone that night. There were strange noises. Empty rooms talk. Too many thoughts demanded our attention.

Years later Mother shared with me the recollections of that day. She recalled sitting in the cathedral alone after I had left to join the tour. She remembered looking up at the altar, the flickering candles mesmerizing her. All had been still, she said, except for the occasional cough and the echo of footsteps on the stone floor. "Gradually I found myself sliding forward in my seat until my knees touched the kneeling board. I hadn't been in that position of prayer for decades, perhaps not since my childhood. My hands came together, my eyes closed, I heard my own voice whisper again and again, 'Please God, bring us together again.' I don't know how often I repeated those words before a strange feeling overcame me. Then through my closed eyes I sensed bright light and when I opened them I saw that the whole church was wonderfully illuminated. I felt as if the light permeated my body. I felt weightless and could not remember getting to my feet. Then I saw the first children coming up the stairs from the crypts and I walked toward them and waited for you. You were the last child, just ahead of the adult group. I saw you squint in the bright light and I called out your name."

Was this a miracle or just coincidence, or does it really matter?

We finally fell asleep. Next morning we gathered our belongings and went down street to the Monopol Hotel for our last meal in Prague. As always we met some Sudeten people with whom we shared our good news. Several women gave Mother notes to take to their husbands in Scotland. Then in the afternoon I shouldered my backpack containing my electric train wrapped again in my new shirts and other clothes. Many years later I would be able to present this toy to my own son. Mother carried the heavy suitcases slowly to the station where they were checked.

At six that evening we joined a crowd of people in front of the doors that led to the emigration hall. Many had come to bid goodbye to members of our group. Then came our turn to enter the hall where we found our baggage waiting. An officer asked us to open the cases, he groped a bit among the clothes and then was finished. We were pleasantly surprised because we had heard rumours about officers confiscating valuables from the travellers. Our passports were checked and we were sent out onto the station platform. A single coach stood on the track to which we had been directed. We heaved our suitcases on board. There were already some passengers seated. After finding a seat we heard a rap on our window. We recognized Hermine from Aussig, a young woman who had been a youth leader in our town. She offered Mother a mug of Pilsner beer with a big head of foam. Mother accepted it through the open window and downed it with great relish. I laughed to see the foam dangling from her chin. Somehow Hermine had gotten past the guards to the platform to see us off. She and the man she was to marry, one of the leaders of the RW in our area, still had many weeks to wait for their escape.

In the meantime, I had been looking around the coach and discovered a boy my own age. His name was Fritz Schneider. His father, who had been the mayor of Graupen, a small town not far from Aussig, had left with my father. His older brother, Herbert, and their mother sat together. Fritz and I were to become the closest friends. Soon others boarded, some of whom we knew such as Gretl Arnberg and her daughter, Liesl, who also became a longtime friend.

We sat in our coach for several hours. Close to midnight it was attached to a train for Moravska Ostrava. The coach was then officially sealed until its arrival next evening in Gdynia. The train began to move out of the station. I looked out into the night and fastened my eye on the red light of the radio beacon on the other side of the city. I tried to keep it in view as long as I could and wondered when I would see it again. I would have to wait for thirty years.

The route of our train followed the new border and indeed at one time crossed Sudeten territory. I saw a large swastika outlined in lights, it sent shivers up my spine. Mother and I took our coats and huddled in them. I fell asleep. When I awoke it was daylight. Mother informed me that we were already in Poland. The new system of refugee transport that my father had written about was in effect; we would not have to change trains or walk through the hills. This same process was followed with transports of refugees every two weeks until 12 March.

On that day Hitler's army was about to invade the rest of Czechoslovakia. The last refugee train left at midnight. The city was in a panic. The news was that the German army was on its way to Prague. Wenzeslaus Square was a scene of great turmoil with men pleading for weapons to defend their country. Volkmar Gabert tells the story of that trip. He was in his late teens and was leaving with his family. He still had a few moments to observe what was taking place on the famous square before boarding the train. Next morning the train pulled into Moravska Ostrava and as they looked out of their windows they saw to their horror that the German army was there ahead of them. The passengers were filled with fear. The train came to a halt. The transport was escorted by a British official who jumped from the coach and confronted the German officer on the station platform. A machine gun nest stood menacingly on the roof of the station. The refugees felt helpless.

The officer screamed at the British official, "Who are these?" and he quickly answered, "They're all Jews."

"Get those pigs out of here," the German officer yelled. With that the train moved out of the station and soon crossed the bridge to Poland. A few moments later, the story goes, a phone rang in the stationmaster's office. The call came from Berlin to halt the train and arrest all passengers, but luckily it was too late. Our transport four months earlier was spared such terror.

All day our train rolled northward through Poland. There was snow on some of the higher ground. By evening we approached the "German Corridor," a strip of land that joined Germany and East Prussia. We had to cross enemy territory once again. The refugees were tense. Would the train be halted, would there be some attempt to take us off the train? In minutes we had passed through the corridor and we breathed a corporate sigh of relief. The train arrived in Gdynia where we were transferred to a bus that would take us to the harbour.

It was dark as we approached the pier of the Balt Line where the *Baltrover*, a passenger carrying freighter, awaited us. We were relieved to see that it was flying a British flag. It was the same ship that Father had been on. We climbed a rickety ladder along the side of the ship and boarded. The vessel seemed enormous, at least compared to those Elbe steamers our family had travelled on to Leitmeritz on Sunday excursions. We were assigned to a cabin for six people. I was disappointed that neither of my new friends was to share our accommodation; however, Mother knew the other four and one was from Aussig, a young woman who quickly befriended me. The other three were a mother and her two older teenaged daughters who were both quite attractive and quickly caught the attention of the crew. Before we left that night, a sailor brought one of the daughters a bowl of sliced pineapple which she shared with me.

I was soon asleep in my upper bunk. It had been a long and exciting day, indeed, an exciting time since leaving Prague. When I awoke next morning we were already at sea. I quickly got dressed and headed out onto the deck. On the horizon, land was still visible. I began to sense the movement of the ship as the swells of the Baltic Sea increased in size. I lost my appetite although I did go to the dining hall for breakfast. What I beheld did not enhance my well-being, particularly the white bread or "fog" as we came to call it. It was tasteless and soft and could not hold the butter. I longed for the hearty rye bread or crusty buns we were accustomed to back home. By noon most of the passengers were suffering from seasickness. It was not a good day but we were on our way to safety.

The following morning as I peered out of my porthole I saw land close at hand. The ship was moving into a bay. We were all dismayed to learn that we were in the Bay of Kiel and that we were once more to cross German territory. Just before we entered the canal we passed a huge battleship that rested at anchor. It turned out to be the famous *Graf Spee* that we would read about later during the war.

Officials boarded our ship. Once again we saw those dreaded uniforms with the emblem of the eagle holding the swastika. Word was passed that we should remain unobtrusive and not rouse suspicion. I have no idea whether those officials knew the nature of the cargo, at least the human freight. We had among us also a group of Polish Jews whose ultimate destination was the United States. All of us trusted that the British flag was our protection and that we were not important enough to precipitate a diplomatic incident. But then, who knows... In fact one of the transports was forced to stop at Danzig where a very much wanted refugee was removed and taken to a concentration camp.

All day we travelled through the canal and at evening entered the North Sea. As the lights of shore grew dim and Germany faded into the distance, we gathered on deck and sang our songs. It was for me the last view of continental Europe for a very long time.

The North Sea lived up to its reputation especially since this was the last week of November. It was cold and the waves were huge and crashed over the bow of the ship. Of course, we were all terribly sick. Mother abandoned me and walked around and around the deck. She managed to keep well.

When I awoke next morning all was still. From the porthole I saw nothing but a wall of real fog. We were now in the Thames estuary waiting for the tide to come in. Gradually, through the course of the morning as the fog thinned, we saw that we were not alone; other ships lay at anchor all around us. By noon we got our first view of English soil. The anchor chain rattled and the engine throb could once again be felt. This portion of the trip was much more pleasant. There was much to see–docks, tug boats and other large vessels and, at one point, the Greenwich Observatory was pointed out. The chief steward of the ship served drinks to the passengers as we crossed the 0° meridian. Towards evening as a soft drizzle fell on us, Tower Bridge loomed up ahead. The drawbridge rose and we passed through. A tug nudged us into a pier and we prepared to disembark.

There were some people waiting for us on the dock,

among them the husband of one of our group. Herr Reitzner waved to his wife but she scarcely recognized him, he looked so thin and old, his cheeks were sunken in. Then she recalled the note she had received from him prior to her departure from Prague warning her to remove her false teeth if threatened with seasickness. Obviously he had written from personal experience for somewhere at the bottom of the North Sea a set of dentures was flashing smiles at fish.

As soon as the gangplank was in place, a flood of reporters with flash cameras surged on board to photograph and interview the first women and children refugees from fascism. I was wearing a rain cape but to prevent it getting tangled in the ropes and cables and other obstacles on deck I raised the tail of the cape over my head. When a reporter approached me I quickly pulled it down, however, I was right away told to put it back where it had been, it looked so much more dramatic that way. I am not sure what they expected from us.

It was time now to step on British soil, safe at last, but far from home in a place where we did not know the language. We had, however, a feeling that we were among a people who cared about us and had some appreciation for our lot. Britain had become a haven for many who had fled from Hitler. A great deal of preparation had gone into this action to save our people. Chief among the helpers were Doreen Warriner and her secretary, Margaret Dougan, Beatrice Wellington (a Canadian) and especially Robert Stopford. They worked tirelessly to clear away the bureaucratic hurdles. Even after the Germans had taken the rest of Czechoslovakia they continued their efforts to rescue as many of the endangered Sudetens as possible. The Lord Mayor of London set in motion a fund to help look after two thousand refugees who came to Britain's shores.

CHAPTER EIGHT

Scots Wha Hae!

Sudeten refugee entertainers
at Dollarbeg, Scotland, 1939
(Author at front, centre)

Scots Wha Hae!

Scots, wha hae wi' Wallace bled,
Scots, wham Bruce has aften led,
Welcome to your gory bed,
Or to victorie!"
Robbie Burns (1794)

The story of the flight of the Hebrew slaves from imprisonment in Egypt was probably not familiar to many of the Sudeten refugees although among us was a goodly number of Jews. Few if any practiced their faith or had any sense of belonging to that tribe whose ethnic and religious identity was shaped by that perilous flight across the Sea of Reeds so long ago. That flight, however, did not remain unique in human history. Today, we can see in the Exodus of biblical fame and the exodus that I experienced as a child as a common theme: the quest for freedom. Our exodus led to Scotland, home of Wallace, Bruce and Robbie Burns, all men who loved and defended their people's freedom with sword or pen.

Our parents craved a homeland and when it was taken away, the doors of Britain, France, Sweden, Denmark and Finland were opened to receive them. They were looking for a temporary refuge until the course of history would change and Hitler and Naziism would be defeated. Perhaps in three years, we thought, we would be able to return again to continue to work for a free and democratic Czechoslovakia, a country where minorities–be they Magyar, Ruthenian, Slovak or German–would be honoured and respected. These German social democrats were dedicated to working out this relationship peacefully but vigorously. In the country that had been carved out of the Austro-Hungarian empire at the end of the First World War, minorities, especially the Germans, had experienced certain disadvantages, as I have already mentioned. They sensed the movement to "Czechisize" the country and they resisted and demanded their rights in areas where they dominated ethnically. They were, after all, three and a half million in a country of thirteen million.

Socialists are by and large an internationally oriented people. They have an intensely held belief in the brotherhood/sisterhood of all working people globally. They uphold human dignity and believe that the fruits of labour should be shared equitably: there should be no major distinction between those who work and those who manage.

When the Spanish Civil War broke out in 1936, social democrats from all over enlisted in a foreign legion to help the Republican forces of that country fight against Franco's fascist regime. They joined with contingents from other countries such as the Mac-Paps (the Macdonald-Papineau regiment) from Canada, a group that was much maligned, even outlawed for many years, by the Canadian government. There were many casualties in that terrible conflict in which Canadian Norman Bethune was deeply involved. The Spanish Civil War was in a very real sense a testing ground for Hitler's war machine. The Spanish Republicans lost and as many of the Canadaian foreign legion supporters as could returned home to Canada while others went to Czechoslovakia where they were once more in flight.

A large majority of the Sudeten social democrats did not

make it out of the country. As many as eight thousand of them ended up in the Dachau concentration camp alone. Some believed ardently that they must stay rather than run for their life. Leopold Poelzl, the former mayor of Aussig was one of them, a brave man who was imprisoned at Theresienstadt (Terezín), the prison that Mother and I passed shortly after we had crossed the provisional boundary between the Sudetenland and the remainder of Czechoslovakia. Several thousand members of the Republican Guard (RW), labour leaders and active party members were rounded up, brutally interrogated and imprisoned in the notorious concentration camps, many of them never to return again. Most Sudetens, even if they had been party members, managed to live quietly, keeping their hopes to themselves until a time when the tables might be turned.

My parents and I were among the lucky two thousand who made it across the sea trusting that Britain would soon recognize the error of appeasement à la Chamberlain. We were fairly certain that the time would come when the Allies would have to take a stand against the fascist powers of Germany and Italy. I doubt that any of us had any sense of the cost of that confrontation. We were nevertheless sure of the final outcome. Hitler would be defeated and our social democratic brothers and sisters in the German Reich who had been among the first to suffer the whip of fascism would be liberated to form a free and democratic Germany. That country would then take its place in a free European community.

Neither we nor anyone else could guess about such a phenomenon as the Iron Curtain or that following the war there would be a forced exile of more than three million ethnic Germans and the end of the hope for a truly multinational Czechoslovakia based on the Swiss model.

On that November evening, with a typical English

drizzle falling upon us we set foot in a land that stood for freedom even though we felt deeply betrayed by Chamberlain and his government. We trusted that because Britons never had been slaves, as the song "Rule Britannia" declares, they would harbour us who fled from slavery.

We boarded a bus that was waiting at the dockside and then were taken across Tower Bridge. As we passed the infamous Tower of London we were reminded of its awful history. Undoubtedly there wasn't one among the adults who did not think of Hitler's dungeons and the close call that we had had. We were to spend the first few days at the London YWCA, not far from the British Museum. The Y was an organization that spoke to us of high ideals. The word "Christian" might have given us some pause but here it stood for freedom of the mind, body and spirit and not of a narrow denominationalism or conservative theology. The Y seemed to embody the teachings of Jesus and the prophets of long ago who also suffered imprisonment, torture and death for the sake of human rights and justice.

My parents had not discouraged my interest in religion. Although they had taken me to the atheist Sunday school previously mentioned, they had also introduced me to their former communities of faith, the Roman Catholic and the Lutheran churches. They had bought me a book of the story of Jesus' passion and death. I was fascinated with the recounting of the final days of Jesus, his crucifixion and miraculous resurrection. I have often wondered whether I in fact trusted that story factually. I know I wanted very much to believe it, just as my parents wanted to believe the story of Fidelio in Goethe's liberation opera. Its theme, its symbolism, is what they believed and trusted. Its truth rests not so much in its accuracy as its powerful symbolism. I saw that same theme in the lives of non-Christians like Mahatma Gandhi. We had not yet heard of Christian leaders such as Dietrich Bonhoeffer who struggled against fascism in the

Germany we had just circumvented. At the time of our arrival he was still a student in the United States struggling with himself as to whether he ought to return to be with the Confessing Church which in the Barmen Declaration had affirmed its faithfulness to God rather than the state, a very definite affront to Hitler's rule.

The British, particularly members of the Labour Party and the unions, came to our support, raising thousands of pounds and preparing refugee camps in Scotland and England. Father and his group had been taken to Scotland to be accommodated in a castle called Dollarbeg just east of Stirling. It was built by a megalomaniac who could not pay the taxes once it was completed. It was then taken over and used by the Workers' Travel Association as a rest home for workers and their families. Unfortunately it could not house everyone and so we had to wait in London until another nearby facility was readied to receive women and children. This week long delay allowed us some time in London to see the sights. I enjoyed visiting the British Museum, particularly the section on Egyptology, and was fascinated with the mummies on display. We were taken on excursions around the city. On a bus ride through the heart of London Mother drew my attention to Piccadilly Circus but I was deeply disappointed inasmuch as I saw no evidence of a big top tent. Although we were splendidly hosted I continued to have great difficulty with English food which I had first encountered on our freighter. After leaving the Y we spent a few days at a youth hostel in Highgate. It was there that I had my first opportunity to unpack my electric train. Unfortunately a different voltage caused damage to an electric coil in the engine and it has never functioned since.

We were, of course, anxious to be reunited with our fathers and husbands and looked forward to our departure from London. However before we did so our group of women and children went to the Highgate cemetery to visit the grave of Karl Marx. We did not equate him with the Russian form of communism but with our brand of social democracy. We were in the first instance "democrats." Marx had held a high place of honour in our home; indeed, we had a bust of him in our apartment. One night before the arrival of the Nazis, it and a number of political books were taken from home and hidden by the underground, probably buried. I have often wondered where.

On 3 December, a Saturday evening, our journey recommenced. At six o'clock, a bus pulled up at the hostel and our thirty women and children once again hoisted our baggage and boarded for an overnight trip to Scotland. In the morning we arrived at Carlisle on the Scottish border where we had another one of those ghastly breakfasts of oatmeal. I starved. We passed the famous smithy at Gretna Green and Mother told me the story of the blacksmith who performed weddings. On the outskirts of Stirling we saw the great monument of Robert the Bruce, a freedom fighter whose story was familiar to some of us. In a few minutes our bus entered through the stone gate into the beautiful park that surrounded the castle Dollarbeg. I was not disappointed, it had everything a castle should—a wall and moat and a tall tower with a lookout. I felt I had entered a world of fairy tales.

Father was not there to meet us. We were told that he and a few men had gone to church in the nearby village of Dollar. They were, however, expected back presently. I was told that if I went back down the road, I would encounter him. I found it a bit strange that Father had gone to church, or that any of the Sudetens would be church goers. Nevertheless, I set off in the direction indicated and just as I had been told I saw a group of men walking through the park towards me. I broke into a run and to the cheers of the other men threw myself into the arms of Father. Almost four weeks had passed since I had last seen him when we said goodbyes in that attic in Prague, not absolutely sure when or if we would meet again. Together we walked to the castle where Mother stood on the steps as we arrived. Our trio was once more reunited. Behind us were all the uncertainties and fears. What lay ahead was, of course, unknown, but for this moment, the present was all that mattered.

The kitchen staff of the castle had been given a holiday and several of the Sudetens with culinary skills had taken over their duties. Thus the three of us along with all our friends sat down together in the beautiful dining room to "real" food, that is a good Bohemian meal.

The Dollarbeg castle was located on a hill overlooking the valley of the Devon, a small stream that wound its way through the beautiful Scottish countryside. To the north were the Ochil hills and the site of the ruins of a more ancient castle which was once upon a time the seat of the Campbell clan. At the bottom of the valley was the little village of Dollar, best known as the location of Dollar Academy, a prestigious "public" school (read "private"). The village itself was largely a retirement community and was home to many superannuated teachers, clergy and generally well educated people who, we discovered, had an excellent understanding of the political situation of the time. A good many of them also spoke some German and could converse with us. They often came to visit at the castle and invited some of the Sudetens to their homes.

The congregation of West Church, a free Presbyterian church, showed particular interest in us. The minister, George Logan, became our first pastor. We were invited to their services which I found quite different from any worship I had known. They were, of course, conducted in English which only a few of us could understand. I was a bit disappointed that Mr. Logan wore a black gown but it was complemented by an academic hood trimmed with white fur. The music was quite good. I especially liked some of the hymn tunes, such as "Unto the Hills Around Do I Lift Up My Longing Eyes." It made sense as it reminded us of the hills of home as well as the hill on which we had found our refuge. Mother was often rather teary-eyed during those services. The memory of her family was never far away.

Conversations at Dollarbeg were never dull. The men had little else to do but rehash politics as they reclined in the overstuffed easy chairs before the immense fireplace of the lounge room. Tea was served in the afternoon with Christmas fruitcake, something I had never experienced before and came to like. I recall listening to one rather stout Sudeten as he pleaded with the rest for "just one night when it is over, just one night for bloody knives is all I want." There was a great deal of anger over the various betrayals that had occurred, social democrats who had sought to save their skins by carrying Henlein party cards and at the crucial hour had turned coat and even betrayed some of their comrades. Revenge was in some hearts and I suppose must be understood. That everything would turn out quite differently when it is over, could not be contemplated at the time.

A few days after our arrival most of the women and children were again moved to a hostel in nearby Alva. I was never there but heard unpleasant stories about it. Tensions developed among the residents over minor personal matters. I can only attribute this to the circumstances in which we were living. Every week they were brought to Dollarbeg to be with their husbands for the day. Mother and I and another family, the Lehnerts were not relocated. Mr. Lehnert took on the responsibilities of running the castle, particularly the kitchen. He had been a cook and waiter at one time and was the one who had presided over the Bohemian cooking when we arrived. The Lehnerts had two daughters. Ruth, the younger one, was my age. She became a good friend. Father had his eye out for a job at the Academy teaching German and Mother had been offered a position in the village. This was against the law, it was clearly stated in our visa we were not to engage in remunerative or non-remunerative work while in this country. Somehow we got away with it. Mother was hired by the rector of the academy as a domestic to start right after Christmas. We had hoped to bolster our dwindling money supply. Needless to say, this was a most difficult period for my mother.

The people of Dollar did everything to make Christmas as pleasant for us as possible. We were invited to all kinds of parties in homes and at the churches. The castle was beautifully decorated and on Christmas day all families were brought together. Children received gifts and I can't remember ever having gotten as much clothing, toys, books and sweets. But in spite of all this Mother was most unhappy. She desperately missed her home and family with whom we had always celebrated that occasion. Her unhappiness also rubbed off on me. I sensed her depression and Father seemed helpless. Having studied English in high school he immersed himself in teaching that language to the others at the castle. Those days seemed marred by sadness.

Once again Mother contemplated returning home. She was not alone in this: Alois Ullman returned by air but got only as far as the Prague airport before being arrested by the Gestapo. He spent the war in the Dachau concentration camp. After the war he was one of the organizers of the special anti-fascist transports out of Czechoslovakia.

One day after Christmas Mrs. Rogers, the wife of the manager of the castle, took me down to a shop in the village. I was completely outfitted in the academy uniform, cap and raincoat as well as suit, socks and even underwear. Everything was standard. Shortly thereafter Ruth and I were taken to the school and enrolled in the fourth class. Miss Henry, a tall reddish haired woman, was to be my teacher. She, as all staff, wore a black teacher's gown. The class extended a most warm welcome to me. It was an all boys class as mine had been back home. It was obvious to me that the whole student body had the intention of teaching me English. I didn't have to do the work that the others had to do, nor was I subjected to the discipline that was regularly meted out to my fellow students. I never did find out why certain children were punished. Every Friday morning a roll call was taken and several were called out and then marched out of the classroom. Miss Henry, our teacher, always had tears in her eyes when this happened. It was the principal, Miss Falconer, who administered the punishment. After a while the boys returned to the class rubbing the palms of their hands, indeed, some of them were rather red around the eyes. When I told my parents about this practice they were rather disappointed inasmuch as they did not believe in corporal punishment.

Each morning Ruth and Dinah, the daughter of the manager of Dollarbeg, walked with me down the driveway that led to the highway where we awaited the bus from Dunfermline that took us to school. There were other students on the bus. One in particular, Angus, became one of my best friends and I continued to correspond with him after I left for Canada. There was one part of the daily routine that I hated with a passion. It was the morning milk break. Each day in mid morning all of the children went to the refectory to have a mug of hot milk. There was invariably a thick scum on the milk and I had to fight to get it down without gagging. I don't think I ever finished it. I had a strong feeling of support from all the children in that school and was proud to call myself a Dollar boy.

Each noon I joined my mother at the home of the rector just off the campus. It was a gray stone building surrounded by a beautiful garden. A bronze plaque by the door had the rector's name inscribed on it. One of Mother's duties was to polish this shiny sign. Mother instructed me to come by the back door and the two of us had lunch in the kitchen. She looked terribly depressed and usually could not fight back her tears when I left. Her employers had hoped that she would wear the traditional costume of the domestic, a black dress and white apron and a little cap, but Mother refused. It seemed terribly degrading to her. The Bells had two small children who came to love my mother because she played with them although they were really the responsibility of the nurse who had the privilege of sharing dinner with the family. She was a wonderful young woman who took a very keen interest in my mother. She recognized her pain and did all she could to stretch the usual regulations of an English home to include Mother in the family. Sometimes my mother was even invited to sit at the dining room table. The nurse spent every bit of her spare time with Mother in the kitchen even though they could hardly communicate verbally. I have often wondered what became of her, in all likelihood she would have joined the forces when war broke out and become a nursing sister. The only person who was a bit of a problem in that home was Mrs. Bell who simply couldn't fathom Mother's feelings. She was not unkind but in her eyes Mother was the domestic. Harry Bell, her husband, who could speak some German, was most kind and often stopped by my classroom to check on my progress. He was thus able to report to Mother about me, which was of great comfort to her.

Every Wednesday was assembly at the school. Before classes, all the students (several hundred in all) gathered in the large auditorium. The entire staff processed onto the stage wearing their full academic gowns. The rector entered and took his place behind the pulpit to conduct the worship exercises. It was a festive occasion which concluded with the playing of the bagpipes. This was my first exposure to that instrument and I sensed that it was very much part of that rugged environment. One day we climbed the Ochil hills to see the ruins of Castle Campbell. From the top of the hills we were able to see much of the country, we even glimpsed the North Sea to the east and the estuary of the Clyde in the west.

On her day off Mother came to our castle to spend the time with us but it was always painful when she had to return to her duties at the Bell residence. Her employment was interrupted for a week when Mother became quite ill and stayed at Dollarbeg. I believe that her illness was stress related, nevertheless, I was glad that she was with me again, even though during that time I had to share a bedroom with another resident.

Dinah and Ruth became my playmates except on those days when the Alva people, as we called them, came to visit. It was then that Fritz was with me. There was much to explore within and without the castle. In the billiard room in the basement we found a wall panel that moved and discovered a "secret" passageway that led out to the moat. We also climbed the spiral staircase to the tower from which we were able to see a great distance in every direction. During the war that tower became an important radio monitoring station.

The castle also had a golf course and beyond that there was a sheep meadow. Fritz and I had never seen sheep before and were very curious about them. One day we went out to visit them and managed to corner one by the stone fence. We had no idea how dangerous this might be and had armed ourselves with golf clubs. We had no intention of hitting the sheep but that was not how the shepherd saw it from some distance away. Suddenly we heard a shout and turning about saw a man come running toward us. We did not think it propitious to stick around and so leapt the stone wall and ran into the woods. In the course of our flight, we became separated. I walked on and presently came to the highway wondering where Fritz might be. It was my conviction that the shepherd was only chasing us away rather than trying to catch us. I found out differently when a door opened in the wall that ran along the side of the road and Fritz emerged with the shepherd attached to his ear. The man seemed to recognize me and with his other free hand engaged me by my ear. We were escorted to the castle where the nature of our crime was explained to the manager. The shepherd left the punishment in the hands of Mr. Rogers who gave us a lecture on the care and treatment of sheep. We acquired the nickname "Sheep Hunters" by all the residents. We did not receive the corporal punishment that the shepherd would have meted out. Being guests from another country and refugees to boot, we were exempted from such pain and indignity.

Life at Dollarbeg was fairly pleasant. The Sudetens wanted to be able to repay the kindness of the local people and so organized a concert for them. Everyone with a modicum of talent was recruited. Others, like myself, were considered trainable and thus included in the programme. There were some very talented people among the refugees, including an excellent pianist by the name of Otto Frank, who could also play accordion. There were dancers, acrobats and singers. A choir was organized to sing Sudeten songs. Ruth and I were coerced into doing a couple of dances, in one of which we were dressed up as Mickey and Minnie Mouse. The concert was well attended, half of Dollar seemed to converge on the castle that night. The concert ended on a serious note with Father giving a speech about the Sudeten culture and its political roots and our hope for a free Czechoslovakia in a peaceful Europe. I believe it was my father's first speech in the English language. All the Alva people were present and there did not seem to be a dry eye in the house. Following the concert the host and the audience presented us with gifts. We felt profoundly grateful to the people of Dollar for all their kindness and support, particularly the churches, outstanding among them was the congregation of West Church. They gave us a glimpse of a different kind of Christian response, more open and compassionate than we had ever experienced. On our departure from Scotland the Rev. George Logan presented my father with two Bibles, one in English and the other in German. I am still in possession of both and cherish them very much.

My tenth birthday on 13 March was not neglected. I was once again showered with gifts; however, on that day we received the news that Hitler's army had moved into the rest of Czechoslovakia. The swastika now flew over Hradčany castle. The nation was humiliated and thus began six years of oppression for the people of our country. President Beneš had abdicated shortly after the annexation of the Sudetenland and had left for exile in London. After the occupation, he and other leaders who had also escaped set up a government in exile. Wenzel Jaksch, the leader of the Sudeten Social Democrats, found refuge in the British embassy in Prague and then, dressed as a skier, he escaped over the mountains to Poland and then Britain.

Hitler was exposed for what he was and those who had been involved in the betrayal at Munich, Neville Chamberlain especially, were discredited. The British foreign minister pictured with bowler and wrapped umbrella waving the Munich Agreement announcing "peace in our time" was now seen as a traitor. It was evident to all that Europe was headed for war. We hoped it would be short, but this was only a hope. We were conscious of the fact that there was really only one viable army in Europe to face down the Germans–the French. Being traditional enemies, France had constructed the Maginot Line against the German Siegfried line. Britain was unprepared to conduct a war except with its navy. Men were seen training for military duty with broom sticks, as there were no guns available. Father knew that it wasn't going to be an easy or quick victory.

We were soon informed that Britain was no longer content to keep us. The British government was already discussing plans for the relocation of the Sudetens with her colonies, New Zealand and Canada, particularly the latter. Wenzel Jaksch was going to be proven prophetic when months earlier he had intimated in a speech that perhaps Sudetens would find their freedom in the wilderness of Canada. Word came to us that by summer the castle would return to its previous commitment. Families in Dollarbeg and the other refugee camps throughout Britain discussed the alternatives, since only a very few would be able to remain in Britain. New Zealand, which was our first choice for relocation, set some difficult preconditions which we could not fulfill, but Canada was prepared to accept as many as would be willing to come as settlers on farms. Because of the Great Depression, Canada had nailed its immigration doors shut but Britain managed to pry them open wide enough for the Sudetens to enter.

Irving Abella in his book *None Are Too Many* tells of Canadian immigration policy vis-à-vis the Jews who were fleeing from Germany. He records conversations between Canadian politicians urging that the Sudetens should be let in to take the heat off their refusal to allow Jews to immigrate. Thus the Sudetens got in even though quite a number of them were Jewish.

On one of my mother's visits from her domestic job we discussed our future. There was now no longer any consideration of returning. That possibility was totally out of the question. Mother preferred Canada since it was closer than New Zealand. Most of the refugees made the same decision. Shortly thereafter representatives of the colonization departments of the Canadian National and Pacific Railways arrived in Dollarbeg to discuss plans. Mother was the only one to ask a rather practical question of these officials: what was the soil like in the area in which we were to locate? The answer was less than adequate and upon arrival it proved to have been quite misleading.

I was well acquainted with the map of New Zealand since for a time it had seemed to be the most likely place of relocation. Then one day I saw hanging on the wall of one of the lounges at the castle a huge map of a vast country with what seemed like New Zealand loosely attached to it at its eastern end. Of course this was Canada and the New Zealand likeness was the province of Nova Scotia. The location of the proposed settlements was far inland. The map itself gave little indication of the remote nature of these areas, except that it was an enormous land.

Plans were developing very rapidly now. Mother was relieved of her job as a domestic. This was probably one of her happier days. Mr. Bell presented her with a very fine letter of reference which I still have in my possession. All of this took on a very serious note when a medical team arrived at the castle to examine us prior to granting visas. This mass examination gave us a glimpse of the Canadian attitude toward potential immigrants. Canada has been a land of immigrants but most of the people knocking on its doors were farmers, usually poor and relatively uneducated. Sudetens certainly were a different lot. We were urban types although some of us had come from smaller communities. We had all been involved in organizational activities such as labour unions and government services. Many of us were quite well educated.

Our medical examination had all the earmarks of a live-stock inspection. Men and women were separated into different sections of the castle and ordered to strip naked. One by one we were ushered into the examination room. One of my pals from Alva was too modest to take off his undies. After disappearing through the door, it opened briefly again and a pair of undies came flying out. It seemed that all the medical team was interested in was whether we could cough and if our genitalia were in order. I went in with my father and believe that this was probably the first time I had seen him naked. The Sudetens proved to be a rather healthy lot which turned out to be very important in the months that lay ahead.

Dollarbeg became a beehive of activity. Lumber appeared in the winter garden and packing boxes were constructed to hold the settlers' possessions. Shortly after Christmas our relatives in our old homeland had sent us some boxes of essential things such as bedding and clothing that we had left behind. It seems that our pursuers had given up on retrieving us. Now all these things had to be packed into regulation size crates for shipment to Canada.

By the end of March, I left school. I must recognize the warm friendship of my fellow students at Dollar Academy especially my teacher Miss Henry and the principal Miss Falconer as well as Rector Harry Bell for whom my mother had worked.

The transport to Canada was well-organized. My parents, along with Fritz and his family, were to be on the first transport across the ocean. The day prior to our departure many of our new friends from Dollar came to the castle to bid us farewell. Next morning Mr. Rogers drove us and our possessions to the railway station at Dollar. I now had to say a rather bashful goodbye to Dinah and Ruth, who had at times during the past months made my life difficult but they had nevertheless been company and often fun. I was glad to leave in spite of all the efforts that had been made to make our stay as pleasant as possible. I believe that my feelings had a great deal to do with my mother's separation at a very precarious time. As we sat on the train I sensed relief. Once again we were together. Our trio was going off to face new and uncontemplated situations but we were going to be doing it together. Mother's positive demeanor was most evident and lifted my spirits.

In less than half an hour, we were in Glasgow and located in a hotel where others of our group were also housed. In the afternoon we were all taken to a theatre where the Lord Mayor of Glasgow received and welcomed us and wished us success on our new venture. We were now no longer refugees but "settlers." Scotland after all was a country that had sent many of its people to the new land across the ocean. If I had any doubts about leaving they were soon demolished by a film we viewed. It had to do with civil defence preparations in case of air raids. It was a frightening film that was to prove quite realistic in the years to come when Britain came under heavy bombardment. Perhaps having been in close proximity to the enemy prior to arriving in Britain made me anxious to get away as far as possible from what might well become the theatre of war. The following morning our group of thirty families was assembled at the Glasgow railway station. Again some Dollar people showed up to bid farewell along with other Sudetens who were to follow on later transports in three week intervals. We were the first and I enjoyed a sense of adventure. Of course, I was heartened by the company of my friend Fritz and several other young people who had been living in Alva. Our journey to Canada commenced.

A train took us to Liverpool where we arrived in midafternoon. From the train window I could see the cranes of the harbour and the masts of ships off in the distance. We were taken by bus directly to the docks where our ship, the RMS *Samaria,* was awaiting us. I was a bit disappointed when I saw that this Cunard liner had only one funnel. It made it look a bit small for this kind of an ocean voyage but once on board it proved to be large enough to get lost in which happened quite frequently over the next seven days. Our group marched up the gangplank, turning briefly to look back and wave at Willi Wanka and Wenzel Jaksch and other Sudetens who had come to see this first group off to their new home.

There was a flurry of activity on the dock. Passengers and baggage were loaded and at the stroke of four that one solitary funnel gave off a loud blast. Chains rattled, there were shouts, commands, several tug boats responded with sharp hoots and the ship began to edge away from the dockside. The *Samaria* had been pointed inland and now made a graceful turn out toward the sea. All of us were on deck looking back to the land that had been our refuge and the people who stood waving on shore. Then I saw my father turn to face the sea. On his face there was a strange expression of disappointment and determination. With his back to the land Father spoke not just to my mother and to me but seemingly to life itself. "I turn my back on Europe, it is finished for me," I heard him say. The ship gave one long farewell hoot and I went off to find my friends. The new world, still far away, approached. It was the day before Easter.

CHAPTER NINE

Settlers

Sudeten settlers arriving
at Pier 21, Halifax, 1939
(Author at front, centre)

Settlers

And if there should be no room left in Europe
for freedom-loving Sudeten German Social Democrats,
perhaps there might be room for them
on the plains and forests of Canada.
Wenzel Jaksch, Leader of the Sudeten Social Democrats,
Prague, fall of 1938

Britain soon disappeared into a fog bank. Our vessel with its load of "settlers" along with many other passengers bound for Halifax and New York churned its way through the Irish Sea. All night the ship hooted its signal. It was a bit worrisome to me, but at length I fell asleep and when I awoke next morning we were approaching Ireland. The *Samaria* entered a large basin through a narrow channel. In the distance I saw a white vessel somewhat larger than ours with two stacks. It looked more like what I had hoped we would be travelling on. We anchored in Cobh Harbour and waited for a tender to come out to us with more passengers.

By afternoon our ship once more came to life and proceeded out to the Atlantic where a heavy swell awaited us. It only got bigger and soon was having its effect on many of the passengers. My friends and I had gone to the front of the ship to watch the waves send spray over the bow. I began to feel somewhat queasy and lost interest in the ocean. When we were escorted from that area of the ship I went in search of my parents. What I discovered was devastation. Almost everyone I encountered was rushing for either the bathroom or the railing. The dining room was almost deserted at supper time. Gradually over the next days we became accustomed to the motion of the ship and I began to enjoy the journey. My group of friends, especially Fritz, was having a very good time and provided some annoyance to the crew by insisting on invading the first class section. After all, our parents had instilled in us a sense of equality.

Toward the end of that week which began with Easter, the sea became very rough indeed. It seemed at times that we were passing through valleys of water and in the next moment we were perched on top of mountain peaks. I wondered what our ship looked like from a distance. In Liverpool it had seemed very large, in spite of its solitary funnel. We had all been absolutely certain that this vessel of twenty thousand tons could not rock let alone wallow and bob like a cork. Then one day we spotted small fishing boats in the distance. There were long moments when they totally disappeared and I could not understand why we were not going to their rescue. A sailor explained to us that these were boats from Canada fishing on the Grand Banks and that they were used to that kind of sea and that, indeed, they were like corks.

One morning when I awoke I found that all was quiet. The ship was motionless and the sound of the engine's throb had ceased. Our cabin didn't have a porthole, so I quickly dressed and headed up to the deck. I discovered a new season. It was sunny but cold and the wooded shoreline was fringed with ice. There was snow on the ground. Ahead of us lay the city of Halifax with tall buildings and church spires. Little did I think that some twenty years later I would be preaching regularly in one of those places of worship, St. Matthews United Church, whose steeple I had seen thrusting out of the skyline. We had arrived at our destination, at least the sea journey part of it. Awaiting us was another week of rail travel which would be far less luxurious. We would get to feel what many immigrants to Canada had experienced over the history of this country.

Tugs came out to the *Samaria* and drew us into shore alongside the famous Pier 21. By mid-morning we were clambering down the gangplank. We filed past a number of people who were awaiting us to thrust literature into our already full hands. These papers turned out to be Biblical tracts to bring us comfort and solace as we undertook the next part of our journey. Did they know something we didn't know?

After passport examination we discovered that one of our suitcases had gone missing. Father and the baggage master went on board once more to search among the New York bound baggage but returned empty handed. This was a grave loss for us, after all we had so little and had lost so much. We were reassured that the case would be located, and indeed a month later it arrived on the farm. It had sprung open at Liverpool and was put aside to be properly sealed and forwarded on the next crossing. When it arrived it was like being reunited with part of our family.

While my parents were engaged in the search for the missing case I was discovered by a reporter from a Halifax newspaper. I was one of the few Sudetens who spoke English thanks to my three months at Dollar Academy and was therefore a source of stories and information about this first group of refugee/settlers who had just arrived in this new land. The reporter plied me with questions and goodies and when my parents found me I was carrying several large paper bags of edibles for our ongoing journey.

The port of Halifax was very familiar with these kind of arrivals. Many a newcomer to Canada has entered at Pier

21, which has now been made an immigration museum. On the other side of the dock a train was pulled up to receive the passengers travelling inland. We were assigned to a "colonist car." It had bunks and a stove for cooking or at least heating up the canned goods that we had acquired at the canteen in the waiting hall and in the courtesy bags of groceries that were given to us by the railway company. Although the coaches were clean when we boarded, they very soon became filthy from the engine's soot. By noon the boat train was on its way past Bedford Basin, the area where convoys of ships would soon assemble to take soldiers and supplies to Britain.

Canada was still quite cold and many of the lakes and rivers we viewed were in the process of spring breakup. It seemed strange to us who had left a very balmy Britain where trees were in leaf and flowers bloomed in the gardens. We felt as if we had skipped a whole season of the year. The train sounded unfamiliar. It did not whistle but let out a mournful wail as it approached each of the railway crossings which were plentiful at first but became less so as we proceeded inland. I had very little sense of where I was.

One morning, however, we emerged from this wilderness and were rattling across a long bridge over an ice clogged St. Lawrence River towards a very large city. This was Montreal, which at that time was the largest city in Canada. The train came to a halt at Bonaventure Station at the foot of Peel Street. We were to spend the day here. In the evening our colonist car was to be attached to the regular transcontinental train, but now we were to have the day on the town.

I set out with my friends and therefore did not witness the happy encounter experienced by those who went up Peel Street past Windsor Station. Suddenly familiar faces appeared on the street. The train from Saint John had just arrived with its load of Sudeten settlers who had crossed from Southampton on the SS *Montcalm*, a Canadian Pacific steamship. This group was to travel much further than we, to northern British Columbia. None of us had much of an idea what would await us at our final destination. When the story was finally told it appeared that our group, which was being settled by the Canadian National Railway, had an easier time of it than those who were destined for British Columbia where some were to spend the summer months in tents. Their job was to break new land and establish farms while we were to take over farms abandoned during the drought of the Dirty Thirties. Neither group was to find "easy street." Among them were our friends from Aussig, the Weisbach family who had been staying at Margate on the British Channel, the largest of the Sudeten refugee camps. Andrew Amstatter in his book *Tomslake* has given an excellent account of the settlement in British Columbia while Rita Schilling in her book, *Sudeten In Saskatchewan*, tells of the experiences of the group of which my family was a part. The two groups were to spend a day together. Some went to a restaurant but soon discovered they could not enjoy a beer together unless they also bought a meal. The price was prohibitive and so they took to the street and a nearby park. When we returned to our respective trains, it was a farewell for at least three years.

That evening the transcontinental with our colonist cars tacked on behind pulled out of Montreal. Days passed by as we threaded our way westward past the still frozen lakes and rocks of northern Ontario. Some of our group became disheartened at this primeval terrain. The end of the world seemed very close. The same scene repeated itself endlessly until one morning another large city appeared out of nowhere. The terminal at Winnipeg, which accommodated both CN and CPR, was very large and impressed us all. Again we were to spend the day wandering the city streets before our cars were once more hooked onto a train that was to take us northward to Saskatoon. The scene outside our sooty windows had now changed drastically. The terrain was flat as far as the eye could see and most of it appeared to be under the water of the spring thaw. Occasionally we saw desperate shacks that seemed to be constructed of turf. Wisps of smoke coming from their tin chimneys indicated these were "home" to someone.

Saskatoon prepared a surprise for us. A crowd of Germans, members of the Bund, a pro-Hitler organization, were there to "welcome" us and some harsh words were exchanged between our militant social democrats and these Nazi enthusiasts. During the hour long stop some of them challenged us as to why we were coming to this desperate country in the midst of a depression when Hitler was establishing a land of plenty where there was no unemployment. At one point an elderly man with a beard, obviously a Jew, dragged a younger woman, his employee, to us and challenged us to tell her what was happening to his people. Some of our men obliged and told about the persecution that was taking place in Hitler's paradise, that Jewish businessmen had their stores smashed, looted and confiscated, that they were forced to wear yellow armbands with the star of David emblazoned on them. The woman's eyes got bigger as she listened; however, we don't know whether she believed our accounts. These Germans were, of course, our natural enemies who at the outbreak of war would find themselves interned as enemies of the state. Soon we were on our way once more, continuing ever northward. By evening we arrived in North Battleford.

Our colonist car had become home for us, a very dirty home although it had been swept and cleaned in Winnipeg. We spent the night on a siding by the station and in the morning resumed our travels to complete the last leg of our inland journey. By noon we arrived in the little hamlet of St. Walburg, the end of the railway line and what to some seemed the end of the world. At the station a group of dignitaries including an RCMP officer complete with red coat and wide-brimmed hat clambered on board to welcome us. There was some shunting about before the train moved out of the station, past the grain elevators, those unusual structures we had seen throughout the prairies. Just beyond the village the train came to a halt. Nearby in a field stood a number of railway cabooses that had been lifted off their wheels. These were to be our new homes.

Hesitatingly we disembarked from our colonist cars and gingerly climbed down the embankment to a couple of boards that led over a water-filled ditch on the way to the little caboose village. It seemed rather romantic to us children but our parents were somewhat less enthusiastic about this new western reality. Officials from the railway company along with our appointed leader, Peter Schmidt, were in a huddle. Lists were shuffled about and then families were appointed to the various cabooses. Our family was teamed up with Franz and Hermine Jany, also from Aussig. Hermine was the very one who had seen us off in Prague, the woman who had brought Mother her last mug of Pilsner beer at Prague's Wilson Station. She and her husband-to-be had fled together and were married in Scotland. They were one of the last to get away before all of Czechoslovakia was taken by the Nazis. There was also a bachelor, Franz Lepschi, to make up the sextet that was going to be living together in this caboose and later on for several months on the farm out in the country.

For me all of this was a great adventure. I could look out of the caboose window as I lay on my upper bunk. That evening all the settlers gathered together with a great sense of anticipation about the future. We were far from home but free and safe and living in a community of like-minded people. Fritz and Liesl and others of my friends were there. What more could I wish for?

Life at St. Walburg was fun. I found a wooden door in the grass near the railway tracks and launched it as a raft on the deep water-filled ditch that resembled a small lake stretching between the tracks and our village. Of course I christened my craft *"Samaria."* Much time was spent by everybody on a huge pile of old used lumber where nails were pulled out of the boards and straightened for future use. We also made excursions into "town" and bought straw cowboy hats and other supplies. Again the church was there to welcome us and invited us to gatherings in church basements, something quite new and strange for us. We had our first experience of church dinners and found them very pleasant and particularly filling. These meals certainly were a happy change from the austere railway fare on which we had been living for a whole week and the canned food we were now preparing in our cabooses.

St. Walburg, as the name indicates, had a substantial German population. On the main street, a dusty dirt road, were located a large general store, a secondhand clothing business, a harness supply shop and of course a bank. There was also a Chinese restaurant and a grocery store in the village. A wooden sidewalk ran along the storefronts with a railing to which farmers tied their horses. Three red grain elevators formed the skyline of this rustic village at the end of the rail line. The largest churches, all wooden clapboard structures, were those of the Lutheran and the Roman Catholic congregations. There was also a United Church and Baptist Church in town. It was certainly quite different from anything we had previously experienced. From its main street a gravelly road led out of town in a northerly direction to the territory we were later to occupy.

Ours was the first transport of settlers, the next groups were to arrive in three to four week intervals all summer long. In the meantime workgangs of men were organized to go out into the country to prepare the dilapidated farm houses for occupancy. They recalled the desperate shacks we had spied from the rail line. The fund raised by the Lord Mayor of London, England, was now entrusted to the railway companies and with it land was bought and a minimum of necessities were provided. I used to drop by the railway car that served as a distribution centre in our caboose village where the settlers lined up each day to receive their essentials: a butter churn, a pitch fork, a water tub and so on.

Gradually the "houses" out in the country were made ready and one day it was our turn to vacate the caboose and head north. Our new extended family loaded old and new possessions onto a horse-drawn hay wagon and when all was ready we climbed on board this rather precarious load. It creaked and rocked as if it would either overturn or break apart. As we moved out of our caboose village we were joined by two more such wagons. We were cheered on by those who were left behind. We would need that encouragement.

The trip was long and arduous. Soon our wagons swung off the main road, following a set of four ruts which, as the miles went by, turned into three ruts and then into two, often filled with water and very slippery. On several occasions our wagon train was stopped at the foot of a hill and the horses of the three wagons were hitched to one. Then, with great shouts of encouragement to the horses, the wagons were pulled one after the other to the top. The caravan then proceeded onward.

As the hours passed I began to sense the call of nature and whispered to my mother that I would have to respond. The driver of our wagon, a former teamster from the Egerland, heard about my need and loudly stated in the strong dialect of his former home, *Do nitzt olles niōcht, ōa muōōte uk vom Wohn runter ōacha* (There is no other way but to pee from the wagon). With some trepidation, I accomplished the feat that would of necessity be oft repeated.

By late afternoon our wagon turned onto a wooded trail. Woods in this part of northwestern Saskatchewan consisted of poplars, the tallest being scarcely more than three or four metres, although most of them were merely scrub. The area was flat, the fields were interspersed with sloughs or swamps surrounded by heavy clumps of willows. Presently our wagon entered the farmyard of friends who had been settled a few days ahead of us. All came out to greet us as we arrived. We stopped briefly to water the horses which had had a hard day and then proceeded further. With every mile the road became less visible in the scrub and grass.

As we emerged from a wood we saw a group of dilapidated log buildings huddled against the bush. The trail led past them but our driver said "whoa" to his team of horses. "This is it," he told us. The occupants on the wagon fell silent as we took in this sadly rustic scene. We couldn't believe these shanties were to be our new home, the end of our flight from Nazi concentration camps. Then Franz Jany got off the wagon and walked over to the nearest cabin. It had no door or windows, only holes where they might once have been. He was joined by his wife Hermine, Franz the bachelor and then my mother also followed. Father and I continued to sit among our possessions, quite speechless. I saw them stick their heads inquisitively into the cabin, then they cautiously entered it. When they came back there was some discussion among them that I didn't hear with the result that the unloading procedure began. It was carried out largely in silence except for a few necessary remarks such as, "single bed over in that corner, box over there."

The wagon, now empty, departed, and the clatter of harness, the creak of the wheels and the occasional word of encouragement from the driver to the horses faded into the distance. We were now alone in the Canadian wilderness of which our leader Jaksch had so prophetically spoken months ago. I explored around the outside of the house and discovered a semi caved in well. Inside the one room shack Mother and Hermine had picked up courage and attempted to make "home." We were lucky to have such resourceful people. Franz Jany, who had been a mechanic and a real good fixer-upper, proved indispensable. The other Franz quietly went about gathering some wood for a fire. Father was the least helpful. Having reached into a suitcase he discovered his copy of Goethe's *Faust* and reread the Easter morning soliloquy, *Von Eise befreit sind Strom und Baeche* (Streams and brooks are liberated from the winter's ice). It seemed to give him courage so that he too joined the "settlers" as they sought to establish home.

The sound of a motor outside and familiar voices brought us outdoors. Emil Arnberg, one of our people, a former carpenter turned journalist and political activist, had arrived with the supervisor in his half ton truck. They unloaded rolls of tarpaper and sackcloth that were to give us some protection from rain which was even then threatening. Arnberg's presence was heartening. To hear his distinct accent and his outstanding ability with curses even brought laughter. Some of us climbed on the truck with whatever buckets were available and drove to a farm nearby where there was a pump to fetch much needed water. Although the truck moved slowly over the ruts much of the water in the buckets splashed out, mostly on us who were attempting to steady them.

In spite of the unbelievably primitive conditions a sense of humour broke out among us and, by the time the stove threw out some heat and the kettle began to whistle, conversation and laughter could be heard. I was the only child but Hermine who was only about twenty-three years of age became my very best friend. She loved children and knew how to have fun. She made life pleasant for me. The house arrangements were very simple, each couple in opposite corners of the room and the same with me and the bachelor. After a simple supper, pork and beans out of cans I think it was, an attempt was made to light a lantern but all of us turned in really early that night.

Some time later I was awakened by sounds in the pitch darkness of the house. There was a drumming noise on the roof and very soon I felt drops of water on my face. Beds were on the move as we relocated to areas of the floor where the roof gave better protection. Our living arrangements were radically rearranged but who cared.

Next morning proved to be bright and cheerful. We were greeted by the chirp of gophers, those big mice-like creatures that we had already observed from the train windows. It seems we had taken over their abode and there was some resentment voiced by them. Hunting these creatures with copper wire slings became a common pastime for us children.

The supervisor came by again and reassured us that we were to live in this house only until a new one was constructed. It had been deemed to be beyond repair. Nevertheless for the next two-and-a-half years, this cabin was to be my home.

I marvel now at how we managed. Undoubtedly it was the fact that we were together and had replaced the family we had left behind. The bachelor was a real help. He made a bow and arrows a few days later and actually killed some partridge that Mother and Hermine managed to cook. As aliens we were not allowed to have fire arms.

Only a few days after our arrival in Bright Sand, as the area was known, an event took place that might have been the end of my earthly journey. I had been digging a hole in the yard, for what purpose I can't remember, when I became aware of an unusual tiredness. It was only afternoon but I could hardly stay awake. Mother put her hand on my forehead and announced I had a fever. I was immediately bedded down. This is all that I remember. Sparse entries in my mother's diary convey their feelings of deep concern. There was no doctor to be had, only recollections of home remedies and folk medicine were available to us. These worrisome entries continued for some days, "Hanns' fever is very high" and "still no change." Then Franz Jany took over, he virtually threw Mother out of the house and went to work preparing wet sheets into which I was wrapped. Sourdough which was to be used for breadmaking was applied to my feet to bring down the fever. These treatments were not unfamiliar to me; as a child I had always dreaded them but this time I could not have cared less. I was away, far, far away. Then there came an entry "Hanns opened his eyes, the fever has broken." I can sense the relief even in those few words.

The first thing I remembered was strange indeed. There was a sniffing sound and a cold nose poked under my covers. A German shepherd, not purebred of course, stood beside my bed eying me curiously. Perhaps he smelled my sweat. Janys had been away and had acquired a dog. Gradually I came out of my illness, whatever it was. We weren't able to put a name to it, but in all likelihood it was pneumonia. The high fever, we had no thermometer to measure it, had been dangerous and had left me very weak. It took many days for me to make a full recovery and must have been extremely worrisome for my parents. However, recover I did.

In the meantime much was happening on our farm. A team of horses arrived, also a cow and two pigs. Mother had put in a garden. Even back in Czechoslovakia she had had a flourishing vegetable plot that had provided our family with produce. She had acquired seeds in St. Walburg which were now planted. Although the harvest was poor–there wasn't enough water and the green sprouts were soon chewed off by the gophers and rabbits–some carrots, onions and radishes did survive.

It was spring and although there was the occasional snow flurry even in May, the countryside was coming alive. I was free to roam. Wearing my straw cowboy hat I explored the woods and swamps nearby. My best friends, Fritz and Liesl had moved into a similar hovel only about a mile and a half away. Fritz and I spent much time together in the woods. Normally we would still be at school but that would not happen until fall. Of course we were curious about the school we were to attend. It was located just across the road from the shack where they lived. We could watch the children arrive and leave and their recess activities. There were about thirty, we guessed, and of every age. The school was a one-room clapboard building with broad steps that led to the front door. Every morning the children assembled in front of the school and then processed inside in an orderly fashion under the watchful eye of a rather young looking teacher. She scarcely seemed older than the oldest girl. Could she really be in charge of this school? Come fall we were going to be among her charges.

There was also a barn in the schoolyard and some of the children arrived by wagon and others on horseback. Imagine having a horse of your own and riding to school each day! We felt we had made a start in that direction, having acquired our straw cowboy hats. Not every rider had a horse all to himself. At least two girls arrived daily on the same horse, which to us resembled a circus act. They rode bareback, which was an even greater feat.

One day Fritz, Liesl and I decided we wanted to get a better look at these stunt riders. We went down the farm path to watch their arrival, but when we saw them approach we secluded ourselves in the bushes and waited. Presently the horse and riders drew abreast of our hiding place. Perhaps we were not as secluded as we thought or maybe the horse sensed our presence with something other than his eyes, whatever the case our presence was discerned. The horse, we later surmised, could not have been a western horse else why should it have shied from people wearing cowboy hats, albeit made of straw. Its ears flew back, it snorted and deftly danced away. The unexpected movement dislodged the riders who, clinging to each other, slipped from their perch and fell into the ditch across the road from where we were hidden.

We emerged from our hiding place, not to help, we had no idea how to accomplish that. Our appearance, cowboy hats jammed over our ears (the store did not have our exact sizes) further frightened the horse which bolted. By the time the two girls had picked themselves out of the dirt, it was well on its way into the schoolyard and the safety of the barn. The girls, Alva and Bernice, whom we later got to know, brushed themselves off, shot angry glances at us and headed for the stable in order to look after their steed and their hurt pride.

By this time, of course, the whole school yard was alive. Everyone was looking across the road at the straw cowboys. The teacher stood on the top step, hands on her hips. Did she wonder what she was in for come next fall? Would she get us to remove those stupid hats? Feeling somewhat foolish, Liesl, Fritz and I vanished into the brush and snuck back to the farmyard. We found other things to do, make bows and arrows, and stand on the huge manure pile to scan the vista for marauding Indian bands, our cowboy hats thrust firmly on our heads.

One day, a small group of dark-skinned and black-haired children came by our place. They carried a sack and had a shovel. They seemed timid but soon revealed the contents of their sack, seneca roots, which they dug out of the soil. They showed us how to find and harvest them. At the post office/grocery store, the roots were sold for a few cents. It was my first contact with Native people and my first commercial venture.

There are various kinds of screams, at least two I can identify. There is the scream of pain or horror; it begins sharply and ends just as abruptly as it began. Then there is the kind of scream that starts suddenly and then trails off. Like the steam from an engine, it blasts forth and as the pressure diminishes so does the intensity of the sound. It seems to announce a release. It was this latter kind that pierced the air and echoed through a poplar grove on this abandoned farm in northern Saskatchewan.

A few weeks after arriving in this remote setting that had become home for us, Mother ventured from the log cabin to inspect the surroundings that were now our farm. She walked behind the barn, an empty, partly collapsed building unsafe for man or beast. Someone a long time ago had hauled logs from some distance to build this barn. The trees in this area were far too small to serve as logs. The builder had been quite a craftsman with the axe. He had squared the timber and fitted them neatly together, but now the whole structure was rotting away.

It was spring and leaves were bursting from the winter weathered branches. Winters in this northern country were long and severe as we would soon discover. But now all of nature was speaking messages of hope. Grasses and ferns were rising from the ground as if rudely thrust from underneath. We were amazed at the speed of growth.

Mother was alone for the day. Father and I along with the others had gone some miles to another farm to fetch some cows which she would have to learn to milk. She had never touched a cow before.

She had time on her hands. It was good to be alone with her thoughts. She walked slowly along the edge of the woods behind the barn taking in all that was so strange but was now hers, something she found hard to accept. She felt a sense of ambivalence. She was aware of how far she was from her former home across the sea. With the growing hostility between Britain and Germany the link with her family was like an elastic band almost stretched to the breaking point. War seemed inevitable and with that, of course, a total separation.

Her thoughts were often with her mother, her sister and brother and their families. She wished that they too might have emigrated. How wonderful it would have been to have them all nearby sharing the hardships as well as the freedoms offered by this new land. Certainly her brother-in-law Max, a man skilled with his hands, would have been far handier on this pioneer farm than her intellectual husband, though he was learning.

She walked on and at length came upon an opening among the trees that looked as though it might have contained a narrow farm road. From directly behind the barn it entered the woods, no more than two ruts and even these were overgrown with weeds while the space between them was well on the way to returning to the bush from which it had originally been cut. She decided to follow this trail. Occasionally the ruts turned to muddy puddles and she had to resort to stomping through the brush along the side. But she was curious about the destination, where it might lead. She almost felt herself drawn.

The road Mother was following took a slight turn to avoid some willows that formed the edge of a swamp, or slough, as the locals called it. We were constantly amused that roads in this country never seemed to confront obstacles but went around them. Why not, after all there seemed to be unlimited space about. Then the road opened into what must have been a clearing some years ago, now filled with tall weeds and low brush.

She stopped and looked. The road dead-ended. She was puzzled by white objects she glimpsed among the grass. Advancing a few steps further she saw a good many more and recognized them to be weather-beaten bones. There was a whole carcass lying there, the rib cage of a large animal, a cow or horse perhaps.

It felt awesome in this macabre mortuary. Then she spied a skull. She had never seen one before. Obviously the road she had been following had been used to transport dead animals into the woods to be left to rot. Now all that remained were whitened bones.

"Is that all there is to life when it is past?" she wondered. "We too share this mortality."

Mother was not sure about her beliefs. From a scientific point of view she saw no evidence of an after-life, only whitened bones and even these crumbled into dust. If religion, the belief in God and life beyond, could make people decent and responsible, then fine and good, but should we really need such primitive incentives? Surely humankind can rise above such superstition. Thus Mother reasoned as she stood among the piles of bones. But on the other hand she remembered the SS brutality, the horror of concentration camps that we had been fortunate to avoid. The very thought of Father caught in their hands could still make Mother shudder.

But there was another thought, or perhaps it was only a feeling, that presented itself; had she not experienced something unusual, well, perhaps spiritual, at St. Vitus Cathedral in Prague less than a year ago when not only November weather had darkened the sky? The future also had seemed bleak. Her early Catholic upbringing had planted some seeds of spirituality that had lain dormant deep inside her. There were times when they gave slight signs of life, "intimations of immortality" perhaps.

Suddenly she glimpsed something crimson, like a burning ember. There among the grass and scrub, it glowed. It seemed to have discovered her almost as she discovered it. Or had this fiery eye seen her as she came through the woods, perhaps had seen her a long time before and drawn her to itself?

The red eye held her and she held her breath. They confronted each other, the red eye challenging her to draw near. A lump formed in her throat. She was aware of her aloneness in this valley of dry bones. Slowly she advanced across the clearing and then recognized what it was that bound her in this spell.

A scream formed in her throat, pressed out and rang among the trees and bones. The Tiger Lily growing straight and tall between the piles of skulls and ribs dared to announce life among the dead. The scream was long as the pressures of the anxieties and stresses piled up over the months of uncertainty and waiting were vented. Her arms, at first flung in the air, came slowly down and embraced her chest. Her scream diminished into sobs. Her eyes gushed tears that blurred the glowing, crimson flower.

She did not kneel to pray or utter invocations, intercessions or words of confession. They were all there, unspoken, yet most real and clear in this Epiphany.

Many years later Mother confided this story to me. The event had been a turning point in her life, a spiritual awakening, an experience that confirmed for her that she was not alone.

By summer all our settlers were occupying neighbouring farms, the closest half a mile away. We visited each other. Some homes were even worse than ours, especially the one that came to be known as the "Robbers Den," which was a log house built into the side of a hill so that the rear wall was dirt covered by slabs of wood. It was dark and dingy and smelled of rot. Franz Brecht, one of the residents, had been an ambulance driver in the Spanish Civil War.

We soon discovered there was a large lake only about five miles from our farm. Bright Sand Lake was about three miles by six, completely surrounded by sandy beaches and beyond that a thick, almost impenetrable evergreen forest. There were several roads that led to the lake but these were virtually impassible. Trees had fallen across them or grown up between the ruts. The community of Sudetens decided this was an ideal place for a gathering. On the appointed day wagons with our people converged on the lake. The men walked ahead with saws and axes to chop a way through the woods and make a passage for the wagons and the horses. I recall the thrill as I first glimpsed the shimmering water beyond the trees.

It was a beautiful day for the thirty families that gathered. We brought food and drinks, all home prepared of course. We all swam and played in the sand and got badly sunburned. In the evening a huge bonfire was built and we sang our old songs, recited revolutionary poetry and remembered events such as the celebration at the swimming pool in Aussig. Often repeated through the two summer months, events such as this gave us courage and a sense of belonging in this strange land.

During the course of the summer, news was also arriving. Letters came from Europe which always brought on a bout of homesickness in Mother. These contained mostly family news; obviously the writers were concerned that they might be read by the police. The weekly newspapers, *The Family Herald* and the *Western Producer*, which had been sent to us gratis, informed us of ominous events as Germany and Britain and France moved toward hostility. We were not surprised. By August, Hitler was making demands on Poland and this time the Allies realized he had to be opposed, that their earlier policy of appeasement had been ill-conceived. Then one day news reached us that war had been declared. It is amazing how quickly that news reached us in this hinterland. We had no radios. All of us realized there was no peaceful coexistence with Hitler. We awaited a war that would restore our homeland to us. We lived in the expectation that we would be returning "home" again after Hitler was defeated.

With the outbreak of war our communication line with our family overseas was severed and that was painful for us all. We now lived on our own, contenting ourselves with the knowledge that we were far away and safe, away from the violence of the war and political intimidation and oppression.

One evening as Mother and I were returning from the field where we had planted potatoes, Mother suddenly grabbed me by the arm. I was startled. There was a strange look in her eye and I feared that she had finally gone over the edge.

"Do you see those shacks over there?" she asked me.

"Of course, " I said, sure now that she had lost her wits. "That's where we live."

"That's right," she replied. "And they are bombproof. Don't you forget it." This was the assurance that guided us through many difficult times.

School began later in the fall, after the harvest, because children were often required to participate in the work. There were about fifteen children of school age among us. The school in our area was called Pine Ridge School, a romantic sounding name. A few pines stood near the school but certainly there was no ridge. There were already about thirty children in that one room building; somehow we would have to be squeezed in. Emil Arnberg was pressed into service to build extra school desks, the lumber was provided. These double desks were very nice, much better than the old ones that had seen better days and had accommodated several generations. Arnberg had been entrusted with the community carpentry shop while Jany was made the village blacksmith. His big job was to keep the old farm implements functional, a daunting task.

On the day school opened, fifteen of us appeared before

Verna Brown, a nineteen-year-old teacher. Among the
Sudetens, I was the only one who spoke English. Verna
proved to be a resourceful and outstanding teacher. She
divided the Sudeten group into two sections, 3A and 6A,
who were to be integrated into the rest of the school over
the next year. I was in 3A, a year behind where I would
have been back home. Verna now had to teach eight grades
plus two subgrades. Such was her skill and rapport with all
of us that I can scarcely remember one disciplinary problem
in all the time I was there. Each afternoon she read to the
class for at least half an hour from books that were not
readily available in those parts of the country. We all grew
to love and respect her. Besides being in charge of the
school she also had to give a good deal of community leadership. We soon discovered she was in the throes of
courtship and the following year was no longer our Miss
Brown but Mrs. Bannerman.

I walked to school with a group of Ukrainian children
one and a half miles across the fields and through the
woods. The school was a gathering of many different ethnic
backgrounds. Our neighbours were mostly Ukrainian but
there were also Scandinavians, a few Germans, some
French and even some English. The beginning of school signalled a new life, a normalcy we had come to miss. The long
journey had definitely ended in this unaccustomed land.
There was work to be done. Winter would soon come, too
soon.

Another event signalled the beginning of new life. Our
good friends with whom we had shared our one-room house
moved to an adjacent farm one mile away, leaving us three
once again alone. It was a bit of a shock. I missed them
greatly and went to see them often. Soon our small month-
ly cheques would cease to come and we would definitely be
on our own. Settlement was over, we were now farmers in
Saskatchewan.

CHAPTER TEN

Farmers?

Felix delivers cream cans
and Lehnerts to town.

Farmers?

We plough the field and scatter
the good seed on the land,
and what comes up we know not.
It's never what we planned.
Local version of a familiar Thanksgiving hymn

Farmers? Well hardly. Somehow there was a misconception about us. Perhaps the leadership of the Sudeten refugees in Britain bore some responsibility for this. In their urgency to find a place of more permanent residence for us, they might have exaggerated our abilities and background. On the other hand British authorities who wanted to have a place to send us coloured their description of the refugees for the colonial authorities of New Zealand and Canada with whom they were negotiating. These colonial politicians somehow caught the myth that the Sudetens were "fine, small-scale farmers who were ideally suited for Canadian family farms." Without a doubt as immigrants to Canada the Sudetens were unique, different from the stream of other immigrants who had chosen Canada as their destination.

The money that had been collected in Britain for the Sudetens was now given to the colonization departments of the two railway companies. Fifteen hundred dollars had been allocated for each family with which land, household and farm equipment would have to be purchased. That might seem like a small amount in today's terms but it was quite adequate then, if used wisely.

The Canadian railway companies had large tracts of land in the west, thus the Canadian Pacific Railways settled their people in the Peace River area of British Columbia south of Dawson Creek, while the group to which we belonged were settled in the area of Saskatchewan north of the hamlet of St. Walburg, a district that had already a significant number of people of German ancestry.

In an honours history thesis called "Colonizing the Victims of 'Peace in Our Time'", Gillian McGillivray, a granddaughter of one of our immigrants, examined the Sudeten settlement projects in Canada's West. Relying on Canadian Public Archives plus accounts written by members of the settlement group such as Willi Wanka, Andrew Amstatter, Fritz Wieden, as well as Saskatchewan journalist Rita Schilling and others, McGillivray managed to produce a most thorough analysis of the settlement project. It is not an altogether positive story.

McGillivray places a great deal of blame for the hardships endured by the settlers, and the negative social situation that developed, in the hands of the colonization agencies of the two railway companies. She blames them for being heavy-handed in their management and failing to understand the nature of the people with whom they were dealing. For instance, the settlers were kept uninformed and uninvolved in decision making. The accounts were never revealed to the settlers. Bad feelings erupted between them both in the Peace River area and in Saskatchewan. They failed to take into consideration that all of these settlers had held high and difficult organizational responsibilities in the land they had left behind. Many of them had come out of a trade union background. Some, like my father, had held high positions in government. They were often dealt with like little children by the colonization agencies and the farm supervisors who had been engaged to help them become established. There were also discrepancies in the allocation of land, some received farms with clear titles (no debts), others were not so fortunate. Many like ourselves lived in dilapidated shacks while the fortunate few had new houses built for them. All these factors led to tensions within the community and between the settlers and the railway companies and their agents.

The hardships which they now had to endure, the unusual labour they had to perform in extremely primitive environments, caused tensions among the Sudetens. When things went wrong, when essential farm implements broke down which happened frequently inasmuch as the equipment was usually old and faulty, displays of anger broke out. They blamed one another and often their solidarity was stretched beyond the breaking point.

I recall a meeting of our farmers in Bright Sand. They had all gathered on a Sunday afternoon at the unfinished Catholic church to discuss the management of farm implements. My father had been put in charge of organizing the distribution of the equipment, not an enviable task. He had divided the farmers into small groups that would share certain implements such as a seed drill, a binder or a hay mower. It didn't always work out, especially with the constant breakdowns, mostly at crucial times. The meeting became tense. Harsh words were exchanged and finally Father was accused by one of the group of being a "business socialist." The meeting deteriorated into a shouting match in which my father wisely refused to participate.

From the back of the room Mother and I watched the proceedings. Suddenly we saw my father become pale and silent, he folded up his papers and placed them into the worn leather case that he had used "back home." He picked it up and with a sad determination walked down the aisle and left the meeting. The room became quiet. Mother and I remained. She wanted to see what they would do now that Father was gone and with him the records of the implement-sharing programme.

His sudden departure seemed to bring everybody to their senses. As I recall it, his attackers were crestfallen. The remainder of the meeting was devoted to a recognition of what hardships and frustration had done to them. Finally Mother and I also left and were joined by others who felt remorseful. On arriving back home we found Father deflated with disappointment. He had not expected that he would be attacked by his own people, those with whom he shared a social philosophy, with whom he had fled a common enemy. It seemed the last straw had broken. It probably also indicated to him that we could not carry on as farmers.

Our quarter section of land was very poor. Less than half of it was under cultivation, the rest was a swamp and scrubby woods. The house was totally inadequate–it had been built using odd pieces of logs that had been put together with considerable skill. By now, however, the wood had become rotten. The new building that had been promised was never built. All the other farm buildings were in an advanced stage of decay. One winter night we heard a crash and upon looking out of the window saw that the roof of the barn had collapsed under the weight of the snow, luckily only onto the hay that was stored there.

We managed to survive the first year. Then a cream route became available. Father applied for it and was successful. It meant that every Tuesday and Saturday, he had to drive the wagon or the sleigh to St. Walburg. On the way he picked up the cream cans that stood by the side of the road and delivered them to the creamery. The route was in the neighbourhood of twenty miles long as it wound its way past numerous farms. It took about three or four hours to make the trip to the village depending on the weather and road conditions. He was paid twenty cents per can for this delivery. As well, each farmer placed a shopping list on the cream can. After delivering the cream and collecting the cheques from the dairy, Father went to the general store and bought the supplies that had been requested. For this service the merchant gave him a 10 percent credit with which he was able to acquire our own supplies. We had become entrepreneurs of sorts. True, this job took two days out of the week but I doubt that we would have survived as long as we did without it. In the wintertime when cream production was low he only made the trip once a week but it was particularly difficult because many of the roads were high in drifts and oftentimes he simply made his way across the fields.

We had acquired what was known as a caboose, a little house on runners that contained a stove that kept the interior warm. The reins from the horses came in through a slot under a front window which of course frosted up and had to be scraped constantly. It also tended to be a bit tippy and more than once had to be righted. It did make the winter trip a little more bearable. On Saturday evening Mother and I would anxiously wait and listen for the sound of the horses' harness off in the distance indicating his approach through the woods. Occasionally we indulged ourselves by buying baloney in town which we fried up and served with potatoes. It was delicious and reminded us of those days when Father returned from a business trip to Prague bringing with him a special kind of Czech sausage that we enjoyed so much.

Although my parents were very healthy people, on one occasion my father became quite ill with a rheumatic condition and was unable to fulfill his duties. Hermine and I took his place. I drove the horses while Hermine lifted the heavy cans of cream onto the wagon. More difficult was the shopping, particularly keeping the various shopping lists in order. On our first trip some farmers did not get quite what they had ordered. We had to repeat this for two weeks and were getting the hang of it by the time Father was well again. Hermine and I usually had a good time in St. Walburg and treated ourselves to lunch at the Chinese restaurant. This kind of food was a real novelty for us.

Mother was a very resourceful person and always made sure that we had a supply of the essentials at home. One day she proudly pointed out to me the sacks of flour, sugar and salt in our larder. With these at hand and with the milk, butter and eggs that our farm produced, she assured me, we could survive for quite a long time.

I often accompanied my father on the cream route. On one such occasion, Mother stepped on a board that contained a rusty nail. It penetrated her rubber sole and entered deeply into her foot. Not only was it extremely painful but she was also aware that there was grave danger of infection, or worse, tetanus.

She recalled as she sat on the ground extracting the boot and nail from her foot that she had seen a familiar plant in the woods that her mother had told her about. It had healing properties and could be used to make an antiseptic poultice. On her hands and knees Mother crawled into the woods. She found the plant, plucked the leaves into her kerchief and then crawled home again where she applied the leaves to the wound. She never developed an infection and within a week her foot was healed.

We were not alone in our struggle, indeed, all of us were experiencing the same hardships. I can't say that I ever felt a sense of deprivation. My three years of farm life were in fact a happy time. Except for that bout with pneumonia and the occasional earache, a malady that I had struggled with throughout my childhood, I was very healthy. Hermine pulled a couple of teeth for me with her husband's pliers, she also cut my hair for the price of one egg. A number of our families instituted a sort of "Order of Good Cheer." We visited each other on a regular basis to enjoy pot luck suppers and homemade entertainment. It was a lot of fun and strengthened our sense of support.

Robert and Stella Weil were one of our Sudeten couples who had been settled on a farm west of St. Walburg. "Robi," as my parents called him, as well as his wife Stella were physicians. After graduating from medical school in Prague, Robi had taken up a practice in Graupen, a small town near the German border. It was a political hot spot. Weil confessed that he kept a revolver in the desk drawer in his office. When the Germans moved into the Sudetenland, he also had to leave. He was one of the last to get out and attributes his salvation to Doreen Warriner who worked indefatigably in Britain and Prague on behalf of the refugees. Their flight was a riveting story.

Although there was a dearth of physicians in this area of Saskatchewan, Weil was not allowed to practice in Canada. However, in time and with public pressure, he was able to obtain a temporary license to set up a medical practice in a place called Frenchman's Butte south of St. Walburg on the banks of the North Saskatchewan River. It was a rustic place reminiscent of Wild West movies. There was a hotel with a railing in front where cowboys tied their horses when they rode into town for the evening. His income wasn't great and he was often paid in kind with produce or firewood. They had a beautiful pair of riding chaps and two lovely horses, also received as payment, which he often used to get to some outlying farm where his services were needed. He was the first Sudeten to acquire a car, a Chevy coupe with a rumble seat that I often occupied. My friend Fritz and I occasionally spent our holidays with them. We rode horseback, watched the prospectors pan for gold in the sands of the Saskatchewan River and visited the "big city" of Lloydminster where the annual fair was held. His was also the first car I ever attempted to wash.

When Bob and Stella gave up their farm my parents acquired one of their cows and her calf. We had to make a special trip to pick up the animals. We had passengers to take with us. Emil Arnberg had left his farm in search of work in Winnipeg but his wife Gretl and their daughter Liesl remained behind until Emil had found work. The Arnbergs travelled with us in our wagon to St. Walburg where they had to see about the deed to their property at the registry. They arrived early in the morning on foot and we all clambered onto the wagon for the three hour ride to town. The Arnbergs got off at St. Walburg and we proceeded on to the Weil farm to pick up the livestock. The animals were loaded into the wagon and we headed back to the village by way of a shortcut that had been pointed out to us.

The shortcut led over a very high railway embankment across a deep valley. It had been the intention of the Canadian National Railway to extend the track beyond St. Walburg to Edmonton. Some of the right of way had already been constructed but it was never completed. As we proceeded along the top of this embankment we observed a very large boulder which appeared to block passage. The horses became extremely nervous as we approached the rock and then attempted to squeeze by with only inches from the edge. We managed to nurse the team past this obstacle, but when they sensed escape they could not be restrained and took off at a gallop. This frightened not only the three of us but also the cow and calf who shared the wagon with us. The cow's fright was manifested by an extreme case of diarrhea. By the time we reached St. Walburg and the Arnberg family the interior of our wagon was not a pretty sight or smell.

It was evening as we left St. Walburg for the three hour

ride home. The wagon now was somewhat crowded. There was one more stop to be made about halfway home. Father had acquired another horse which was to be picked up at a farm along the way. It was pitch-dark as we tied Ginger, a large dark brown gelding, to the tailgate of the wagon. I perched myself on the gate to keep the horse company. Thus we journeyed on, Father holding the reins with Mother beside him on the buckboard. Gretl and Liesl were seated on a board behind them, the cow and calf took up the rest of the wagon. I was riding on the tailgate with Ginger following more or less obediently behind.

As we drew closer to home we observed a redness in the sky. It seemed to lie directly in front of us. Presently we discovered that we were approaching an area where a forest fire had passed through. It was magnificent. Old trees exploded sending great showers of sparks into the sky resembling fireworks. The fire left the ground scorched and the glowing embers looked like the lights of a large city. At first we feared the worst that our farm had been burned down. Everyone shared the fear including Ginger who tugged at the wagon making progress difficult for the team who were nevertheless determined to go home. Blossom, as we came to call the cow, had a renewed attack of diarrhea. We wondered where it all came from while her calf wailed constantly. We must have been an interesting sight; fortunately or unfortunately, no one was there to witness our caravan.

We soon discovered to our relief that the fire had passed by our farm leaving it unscathed. It was after midnight when we arrived at our destination. The horses and the cow and calf had to be stabled. Happily our neighbours had milked our cows. The wagon was a mess into which Arnberg's briefcase containing the documents had fallen. Unfortunately it had not been completely closed so that some of Blossom's flood had leaked in. At night it was hard to assess the damage. We all tumbled into whatever beds were available. Our cabin had but one room, there was little privacy, but who cared? Next morning we discovered that the documents were still in order although tinged with a distinctly different colour and odour. My job that morning was to dig out the two inches of hardened cow dung that covered the floor of the wagon.

Water was a real problem on our farm. There had been a well but it had collapsed and was considered too dangerous to rehabilitate. It was decided that we should dig a new one. One of our farmers who claimed he could "divine" for water with a willow wand walked all over our yard and decided on an ideal location for the well. A gang of neighbours gathered and began the hard job of digging. Fortunately the ground was very light, mostly sand, and therefore easily removed, but the walls kept caving in. A wooden casing had to be constructed to hold the soil back as the workers dug. They constructed a wooden winch to haul the buckets of earth and sand out of the pit which was backbreaking labour. The resulting pile of sand became my playground. After thirty feet of shaft the diviner's prediction was still not realized. It was considered unwise and dangerous to continue the digging. A "sand point," a pointed pipe with holes in it, was pounded into the sand until there was a show of water. We thought we had succeeded, but our well proved to be quite inefficient. We had to pump eighty times for one measly pail of water. Most of the time we took our animals to the neighbouring Fleck farm to have them watered. Often times the well became dry and my parents were forced to carry two pails of water suspended by a yoke across their shoulders all the way from our neighbours farm, a distance of almost half a mile, which was quite physically demanding.

The well diggers were more successful at other farms. On the completion of one such well the diggers which included my father and Frank Jany held a celebration to which some alcoholic beverages were brought. This beverage, probably home brewed, was quite a novelty given our financial situation. It was in the wintertime and we travelled to the farm by horse and sleigh. The party was a great success. There was lots of food and drink and fun. In the course of the evening there was a loud crash, and to everyone's amazement the homemade rocking chair which my father was occupying, being somewhat unbalanced, had flipped over imprisoning him underneath. It became evident that Father had lost control of his sense of equilibrium. Although unhurt, he felt the need to stretch out on a bed where he fell dead asleep. The party carried on until the wee hours when Mother thought it was time to go home. No one seemed fit to drive the horses except me. The women loaded the men like dead weights into the sleigh through the tailgate. I had become a real farm boy and was able to hitch the horses up and transport this human cargo to their respective farms. Next morning Father had a very bad hangover and Mother was furious with him. It was the only time I ever saw my father under the influence of drink.

On another occasion Father and some other farmers had run out of cash and were forced to apply for social assistance. The "dole" was not uncommon among the farmers in this area, the few dollars thus extended had to be repaid by doing community work. So it was that Father and Frank were told to report to a certain road intersection early in the morning armed with a shovel and rake to await the arrival of the road grader. They waited for several hours. At length they unpacked their lunches and found a shaded spot under some trees to enjoy their meal and eventually fell asleep. About midafternoon they were awakened by the roar of an approaching truck. A heavy cloud of dust came up the road signalling the arrival of the superintendent of welfare as well as road maintenance, a convenient arrangement. He explained that the road grader had broken down but inasmuch as they had made their requisite appearance their debt would be forgiven. He produced a yellow receipt pad, signed two certificates and sent Frank and Father happily home. Years later my father wrote a rather humorous story for a German publication called "The Day I Was A Welfare Bum."

Every story has to contain some sex, I have been told, so this is it. One day we observed Emma, our sow, exhibiting some strange antics. She frolicked about Herman (Emma and Herman, our two pigs, were named after the Goering family) who having been disabled some months ago was showing only signs of polite annoyance. Emma took her rear to the boards of her pen with enthusiastic vigor, a pleasant smile enlivening her snouty face. It seemed to us that her confinement would soon give way.

Our neighbour who happened to be calling one afternoon suggested that Emma needed male attention and indicated that one of the nearby Ukrainian farmers had a boar who could well satisfy her needs. Arrangements were made and Emma was loaded into the box wagon. The whole family travelled along. It was to be my first lesson in sexual education.

For a small price, I think it was a bag of oats, the Ukrainian admitted Emma to the boar which showed little inclination to his task although Emma flirted vigorously. "They should be left alone," our Ukrainian friend suggested and invited us for coffee to his house.

An hour later we returned. It seemed to us that Emma and the boar had become well acquainted and we suspected that she would soon show signs of expectancy. Several weeks passed by with no indications of fulfilment. Emma was, so to speak, still hot to trot. Whatever happened during coffee time had obviously not "taken." A return engagement was organized. Emma once more boarded the wagon.

I think that she must have had some inkling of what was in store for, unlike the first occasion, she readily boarded her conveyance.

The Ukrainian, being seasoned in animal husbandry, understood that often it takes more than just one call. Emma was once more admitted into the presence of her friend. This time the boar seemed much more friendly, affectionate is the right word. They wandered off like some lovey dovey pair. Before departing for another round of coffee I observed the lovers crawling into an opening in the large straw pile.

Recounting this event to some of my classmates a few days later, one of the older boys explained that there was a difference between pigs and humans. "Pigs," he said, "do it best in straw, while humans prefer hay."

This last visit proved fruitful. Emma returned to her placid demeanour and soon showed signs of pregnancy. Our family was delighted. We counted off the days on our calendar for the time of her delivery. Emma became extremely large. The supervisor guessed that there would be at least eight offspring.

We were warned that it would be important to be present at the delivery inasmuch as sows aren't always motherly. Often they even devour their young or while nursing such a numerous litter might accidentally lie down on one with imaginable results. Also piglets, like humans, vary in size and aggressiveness to feed themselves. This often leaves the weakest ones unfulfilled.

As the time drew near we decided to take shifts at watching in the pigsty. This building was the smallest and certainly the worst of our farm buildings. We rigged up a kind of lean-to bed for whoever was on shift. Unfortunately, the blessed event occurred in my absence. My education had not been completed but I hoped there would be other times.

Emma bore a litter of eight, six survived the first forty-eight hours, one other showed some abnormalities in the form of a protruding bowel. Soon, however, we were faced by another problem. It seemed that the piglets were not getting the nourishment they needed. Somehow, I can't remember how, we discovered that Emma suffered from a lack of milk. There was but one way to save the litter and that was to remove them from their mother to our house. Emma quickly overcame her postpartum blues. We then endeavored to feed them with a bottle.

This intimate relationship formed very strong bonds between us and the litter. All of them, including the abnormal one, survived and flourished. One day the supervisor examined it and with his finger, unwashed, simply stuffed the bowel back in where miraculously it stayed.

My education was not yet finished. Some weeks later the supervisor who came roaring by in his red truck suggested that the little males were ready for castration. We were perplexed. Most of us didn't even believe in circumcision. A number of Sudeten farmers were invited to the Janys where the supervisor would demonstrate the trick.

Our growing family was loaded into the wagon and taken through the woods to Jany's farm. A bowl of boiling water was brought out to wash a stiletto, a curtsy to antiseptic surgery. Alcohol was also supplied but I think the supervisor slaked his own thirst first. The pigs from the various farmers were then brought out one by one to undergo the surgical procedure.

I had no great desire to witness all the gory details and thus removed myself to a nearby fence. The Sudeten farmers all stood around in a circle so that I couldn't see what was happening, but I could hear.

Suddenly there was a strange commotion among the men. Something untoward had happened, I surmised. The screams of the piglets had subsided but when the circle parted the body of a man was carried out. I jumped from my fence rail with excitement, rushed over to discover who it was and what had happened.

There was some laughter so I took it that it wasn't all that serious. "Poor Felix [my father] just doesn't have the stomach for this job," I heard Franz say. A glass of water revived him and soon he joined me on the rail of Jany's fence.

At the end of the second year, our trusted friends, the Janys, decided they could do better in the city and departed for Toronto. Their absence left us feeling very much alone. We did not know how we would cope without them. By now there was a steady exodus of "farmers" who, with whatever funds they could scrape together, bought tickets to Toronto, Hamilton or westward to Edmonton, where they managed to get jobs in industry. Quite a few of them had been in the textile industry and found employment in the factories of the east. Some enlisted in the Canadian forces, but that avenue was limited to those under 38. Our neighbour's sons joined the airforce and the army while their parents headed for Hamilton. My folks felt somewhat disadvantaged inasmuch as Father did not have a trade or skill that was needed in this country. But the end of our farming days approached.

By the end of the summer of 1941 it became quite evident that we were facing a crop disaster. Growth was poor and the fields were infested with thistles and wild oats. Although most of our livelihood was provided by our cream route the crop was still vital. It now seemed that we would only barely survive the coming winter. On the day we were thrashing, nine bushels to the acre, which was a virtual embarrassment, a messenger arrived with a telegram for my father. It was from his old friend Josef Bělina with whom Father had worked on the *Aussiger Tagblatt* (*The Aussig Daily News*). Bělina had also escaped to London and was now engaged in a news and information service on anti-fascist matters as well as serving as a correspondent for a variety of publications. The telegram informed Father that his friend would be in Toronto and urged him to leave the farm. Bělina had some contacts in the east, including Thomas Bata of the Bata Shoe Company which might possibly lead to a job for Father. The handwriting on the wall was becoming clearer all the time and so Father decided to seek his fortune in Toronto.

As soon as the harvest was "finished" (that word has several meanings in this context), he gave up his cream route to another farmer. We sold our calves and a couple of pigs and raised enough money for a ticket to Toronto. Mother and I were left behind to wait until Father was established. In the meantime we would wind up the farm, selling everything movable.

Once again Mother and I were on our own. Soon the winter descended on us with a fury. We battened ourselves down in our log cabin and tried to keep as comfortable as we could. We still had a cow to provide us with milk, chickens that laid eggs and roosters that could be slaughtered. Much time was spent searching for and hauling dead trees out of the bush and cutting them up for firewood to keep us warm. The wind howled about our little cabin and the snowdrifts obscured our windows. Every morning the water bucket was frozen solid.

Nevertheless, we had plenty to eat. Every morning I went into the woods to check my snares for rabbits and we often had a delicious stew made from those lovely little bunnies. There was another strange phenomenon that supplied us with fresh meat. Each evening the prairie chicken settled into the snow on the field. Over night their feathers froze into the snow and if I got out to the field early enough I would have my pick. I simply needed to pull them out of the snow and wring their neck and bring them home. By nine in the morning the sun thawed them out and they flew off. I wasn't the only one who benefited, there were coyotes and wolves about who shared this manna from heaven with us.

Father's first letter from Toronto was encouraging. Although he had missed his friend Josef Bělina, he was able to follow up on at least one lead. He had an interview with one of the executives of the Bata company who guaranteed him work upon completion of a machinist course at Central Technical School in Toronto. With that proviso he was able to get into the night school which had been established to train workers for the war industry. The night school students received a small remuneration from the Canadian government to tide them over until they were employed. Father was living with the Janys in a house that was rented by the Weisbachs who had also fled from their farm in British Columbia.

We were to join Father in Toronto as soon after New Year's Day as was feasible and so we were faced with spending Christmas alone. We would really be alone inasmuch as most of our friends and neighbours had also departed for the east. Mother and I made the best of it. We had a small Christmas tree which we decorated with aluminum foil that we had saved up from packages. Mother managed to bake some cookies which we strung up on the tree. Most important for our morale was the annual Christmas celebration at the school, an event which all the community attended. For weeks the children had drilled songs and skits and presentations for this occasion. The finale of course was the arrival of Santa Claus who had a gift for everyone.

A money raising event early in the fall had gained a sufficient amount of money to allow each child the privilege of choosing a gift from the Eaton catalogue, up to seventy five cents, I believe it was. The collective order was sent off to the Eaton mail order store in Winnipeg who sent the gifts individually wrapped and labeled to the school. I had chosen a book, *The Adventures of Huckleberry Finn* by Mark Twain. I had read *The Adventures of Tom Sawyer* in German back home and enjoyed it immensely. For many this was the only Christmas gift they would receive. After the celebration a dance took place at which three local musicians (I use the term loosely) provided the music.

School had ended early that year because of the bitter cold and snow conditions. We hastened between the cabin and the barn to do the chores. It was virtually impossible to spend any time in the open without suffering frostbite. Bedtime came early each evening. It was too cold to stay up. As soon as the chores were done (which were rapidly diminishing as we disposed of our menagerie) Mother and I would have our supper and then get into bed along with our dog and several cats to keep us warm. We pulled a blanket over our heads, stuck the box of chocolates which Father had sent for Christmas between us and turned on a flashlight. In that cozy, tent-like environment we told stories to each other until I fell asleep. It was a continuous tale that was to be taken up the following night by the other person. These fantasies kept us sane and instilled in me a sense of imagination and some skill in storytelling.

At the end of January, Father had written us that we should prepare to join him. By early spring, his course would be finished. We were more than ready to leave. The farmland had been rented out, and the cows and horses had been sold, except for Blackie, my favourite which had been disabled when his foot was sprained in a gopher hole. He would recover but no one was willing to buy him. One of the Sudeten farmers took him off our hands promising to look after him "until I came back again." Blackie was a very gentle animal that I loved and often rode bareback since we couldn't afford a saddle. It was a sad leave-taking. Fifteen years later, I visited this same family in Edmonton who had also left the farm. I appeared unannounced at their door and when Martha Brecht answered my knock I explained that I had come to collect my Blackie. She was overjoyed to see me, but, of course, Blackie had died some ten years earlier. She assured me that he had enjoyed a leisurely retirement in their pasture.

I was truly sad to leave the old log cabin that had been home for us for almost three years. I was devastated when I said goodbye to my two dogs who were taken over by neighbouring Ukrainian farmers. The large wooden box that had been made in Scotland to carry our possessions to Canada was once more filled with what little was left of our possessions, mostly the feather bedding that our relatives had sent us before the war broke out. On the day of departure the farmer who was to rent our farm loaded the box into his sleigh. The remainder of the grain was then poured into the sleigh and taken to St. Walburg. The wheat and other cash from the sale of a variety of objects such as the cream separator was just enough to pay for our two tickets to Toronto.

Before leaving the little village we had lunch with a family who owned a radio. We had not heard one since coming to the farm. It was Saturday afternoon and our friends turned on the transmission of the Metropolitan Opera. It was Puccini's *Madama Butterfly* that was being performed that afternoon, my mother's favourite. Unfortunately we were unable to hear any of it. However, we did hear the American national anthem played as was customary before each of the performances. As the sound of the music, played by a large orchestra swept over us, Mother broke down and wept. My parents had been great lovers of classical music and this was the first time in many years that she had heard a full orchestra playing. We departed for the railway station where three years earlier we had arrived. That event seemed so long ago, as if an entire age had passed.

Uprooted and Transplanted

It was a very cold winter day as the train pulled out of St. Walburg on its way to North Battleford. The engine's wail that we occasionally heard from a distance on the farm now indicated the end of our farming days.

We stayed overnight in North Battleford with Everett Baker, the representative of the Saskatchewan Wheat Pool who had been a faithful visitor to our farms and a great source of encouragement to all of us farmers. He was also an avid photographer and left quite a collection of excellent colour slides of the Sudeten settlement. These can now be found at the Saskatchewan Public Archives.

It is debatable whether the Sudeten settlements in Saskatchewan and British Columbia were a success or a failure. There are still Sudetens in both locations, in some cases their children and grandchildren have carried on and enlarged their farms and have become more successful than their forebears. More than that the Sudetens, whether they departed or remained, have left their imprint on these communities, more so in the British Columbia settlement than in Saskatchewan.

In August 1989, the Sudetens celebrated the fiftieth anniversary of their arrival in Canada. They came to Dawson Creek from many parts of this country. There were also visitors from Germany who had survived the war and its aftermath. One of the highlights of the reunion was the unveiling of a statue in the community of Toms Lake where the original settlement had been established. It depicts a father, mother and small daughter in rather un-Canadian "city" clothes with an old suitcase standing between them looking towards the woods. On the pedestal of the statue are the names of all the settlers who had come from the Sudetenland of Czechoslovakia to this country.

On the evening of the banquet, Rita Schilling (who had just published her book, *Sudeten In Saskatchewan*) and I discovered that there was another gathering of Sudetens near-

162

by. We visited this rather large group and found these were the grandchildren of the original Sudeten settlers. Only a few spoke German. They were having a most enjoyable time telling the recollections of their youth on the farms. What really amazed us was the religious faith of these young people, evident in their stories and songs, albeit somewhat too evangelical for our theological tastes.

The farming experience was undoubtedly a time of transition, a crossing over, with much hardship and pain. But it was a passage to something else. Perhaps it made us truly Canadian inasmuch as we encountered what so many other newcomers to this land had experienced.

From the Peace River area of British Columbia and the settlement in Saskatchewan, we were once more dispersed all over Canada. The hope to return to our native Czechoslovakia after the war was beginning to fade. We were becoming Canadians. Sudeten clubs were established in many of the large cities where the former farmers as well as emigrants from Czechoslovakia after the war meet periodically to recall their memories, to sing the old revolutionary songs and to stand in solidarity with one another. As a minister in Toronto, I was occasionally called on to celebrate the lives of a number of these people who ended their mortal journey in this new land. Among them have been my own parents, my father, Felix, in 1985 and my mother, Gertrude, in 1995.

There is no doubt in my mind that these Sudetens are a very special people with a high sense of idealism. Theirs was more than a scramble for their own survival or well-being. Their political convictions of freedom, human rights and social justice continue to be deeply held and have added to the strength of the Canadian political scene. Some have rediscovered their Jewish roots in the synagogues of this country. Many others have found a spiritual home in the churches of this country, particularly the United Church of Canada, whose emphasis on social justice rings a familiar note.

Chapter Eleven

City Folk

Batawa homes, 1942

City Folk

Tower'd cities please us then,
And the busy hum of men.
John Milton: L'Allegro

After a long train ride through the frozen forests of northern Ontario, the ice-coated train wound its way down
Toronto's Don Valley and entered the dark interior of
Union Station. The train was crowded mostly with men and
some women in the uniforms of the branches of Canada's
military forces. In Winnipeg we had been joined by the
Schneider family. Fritz and I kept each other company
which made the dreary journey a lot more pleasant. They
were on their way to Hamilton where Willi (who had once
been the mayor of Graupen) had found work in the textile
industry. A short trip from Toronto to Hamilton still awaited them while we were almost "home."

We joined the stream of passengers moving down a
labyrinth of passages to the huge waiting room. A large
audience stood on either side of the exit looking for familiar
faces. Mother and I scanned the crowd but unfortunately
no one was there to meet us. The Great Hall was crowded
and I scurried around among the people to locate my father
but returned disappointed to where my anxious mother was
waiting and guarding our few pieces of baggage. When the

crowd had dissipated somewhat we heard a shout and saw the Janys and my father come hurrying down the ramp toward us. Once more we were reunited although Mother was somewhat miffed by their delay.

As we came out of the cavernous station I was confronted by my first glimpse of a skyscraper, the Royal York Hotel and beside it the Bank of Commerce which, until many years after the war, would dominate the skyline of Toronto. I was impressed but I was never so cold as that morning waiting for the streetcar in the icy draft that was sweeping up from the lakeshore. In Saskatchewan it had been bitterly cold but the dampness from Lake Ontario penetrated painfully.

We took the streetcar, another novelty, and arrived at Muir Avenue, the home of the Weisbachs and a number of other Sudetens who had been shoe-horned in. It seemed almost like home to see all those familiar faces and hear their Sudeten dialects. Needless to say the house was crowded but we were surrounded by friends. Father was still at his night course which was soon to be completed. Of course we would not be able to continue to live with the Weisbachs and went in search of a new location. In the meantime I undertook to explore. With a city map in my pocket I set out on foot.

My first trip on my own was to the Eaton store at the corner of Yonge and Queen. I had known about this company from the mail order catalogue that was essential reading on the farm. However this store was something else, a veritable mecca for me. I was mostly interested in their book section although I could not buy anything, I had almost no money. I spent my time just walking and looking and being introduced to a new life. I strolled through the furniture department and saw objects that had been factory produced unlike the primitive homemade benches and tables we had left behind in our cabin in Saskatchewan. I was also somewhat overawed by the well dressed sales personnel. They looked wealthy and very English.

Toronto was in the midst of the Second Victory Bond Drive. A large structure in the form of a thermometer was attached to the central tower of City Hall next to the giant five-storey Eaton store, showing the amount of the contributions that had been received. I watched parades and heard speeches exhorting people to give for victory. There was something a bit strange about all this. I knew that the war was being waged against the forces of Hitler who was our very personal enemy, the very reason for our being in this country. But there was something else that bothered me, I was German and German was my mother tongue. I saw caricatures of monocled German officers. Although I was born in Czechoslovakia and was a citizen of that country and included in my parents' Czech passports, I could no longer speak that language. As I watched the soldiers marching I wondered whether they had any sense they were to fight to liberate my country. Had they even heard of the Sudetenland? I recalled the ambivalence that I had experienced as we fled from Aussig to Prague. I was then considered a German and therefore held suspect by many Czechs. This sense of being an outsider, of not belonging, has pursued me much of my life.

There were, however, people in this city who understood my parents' ethnic and political situation. We were to meet them at the University Settlement House. Many of the Sudetens were invited to evenings at this club for university people who had some appreciation of our lot. Indeed, some had been in touch with us in Saskatchewan and had organized clothing drives to help us. Two women, Miss Hamilton and Miss Ray had even come to visit our settlement and knew first hand of the primitive conditions in which we had lived.

We were welcomed to their gatherings where there was

usually some sort of programme, a lecture or, on one occasion, a singer who sang Schubert lieder in German. This was followed by refreshments and conversation in which I as a thirteen year old was included probably because I spoke English better than the others. It gave us a feeling that we were understood and our lot appreciated. At that point in my life I had no expectation that I might someday go to university. I am curious about who might have been at those parties, undoubtedly they were well informed people whose names might have been familiar in Canadian academic circles.

Three weeks after arriving in Toronto we moved to a new location near Davenport and Dufferin. Again we moved in with another Sudeten family renting a small house on Bristol Avenue. We took two rooms and a kind of a summer kitchen where we had a hot plate and an ice box. My parents had also bought a few odd pieces of furniture from the second hand store run by the Crippled Civilians. Once there I was enrolled in grade six at Regal Road Public School.

Mother had in the meantime begun working at the Devonshire Clothes factory sewing buttons on uniforms and was actually earning money. Father, who was at night school, accompanied me to my new school. The principal took me to my classroom and introduced me to Miss Sloan who was to be my teacher. Before taking me into the classroom Miss Sloan asked me an important question. "Hanns," she said, "as you know we are at war against the Germans and the name Hanns might cause you some unpleasantness, are you sure you want to go by that name? We could use the English equivalent John, but I must warn you that there are already two Johns in the room."

It didn't take me long to decide that I would take my chances with my original name and thus was taken inside to meet my fellow classmates. To my relief my name never caused any trouble even though I still had a fairly strong German accent which must have reminded some of them of those awful German soldiers depicted in the comic books that everybody was reading: "Ve hev vays of making yuh tock."

The room was different from any classroom I had ever visited. The pupils sat at tables, one at each end and two side by side looking forward toward the teacher's desk. Each table was a team and functioned together in competition with other table groups. The day began with mental arithmetic which I had never done before. I was an abysmal failure and a drag on the rest of my table mates. But there were other subjects in which I shone. On one occasion the class was to make presentations on various aspects of the war. I was given the assignment of reporting on the Commonwealth Air Training Plan. I knew nothing about this but found that the *Canadian Geographical Journal* to which we had a complimentary subscription had carried an extensive article on that very subject. I worked very hard on it and when it came my turn to make the presentation I absolutely amazed the class and the teacher. Miss Sloan took me aside after classes to quiz me as to whether my father was a spy, but I was able to reveal my sources to her and received great compliments and a high grade for my table.

On another occasion we were to learn some wartime poetry. I memorized a well-known poem about flying which I liked very much. We were asked to recite the poem from memory and I gave it everything I had as I recited: "Up, up the long delirious burning blue, I topped the windswept heights with easy grace and flung my eager craft through footless halls of air...put out my hand and touched the face of God." Miss Sloan was ecstatic with my performance and arranged to have me perform the poem in several classrooms and also before an assembled group of teachers.

Once again, my table benefited greatly.

My big problem was mathematics in which I did very poorly. One day my teacher asked me whether I would be terribly upset if I failed my year. In those "good old days of education" when you failed one subject you repeated the whole year. It should not have been too surprising since I had changed provincial systems, had only recently become fluent in English and had missed more than three months of schooling that year. Tearfully I admitted that I would be greatly upset. I graduated that spring.

One day shortly before the end of the term Miss Sloan invited me along with some of her former pupils to her apartment for supper. In the course of the evening my host once again took me aside and asked me, "Hanns, are you Jewish?"

"No," I answered a bit startled by her question although I recalled that there were a number of Jews in our Sudeten group.

"I am so glad," she said. "I don't like Jews." This wasn't altogether surprising to me for I had already noted evidence of anti-Semitism in Toronto. I had seen quite a number of signs in stores and restaurants "Gentiles Only" and even more bluntly "No Jews."

One Sunday my mother and I were visiting another Sudeten family who lived in the College-Spadina area. They had a boy two or three years younger than I. We went out to play in the back alley when suddenly we found ourselves surrounded by a gang of boys. The one who seemed to be their leader approached me and grabbed me by my arm. "Are you Jews?" he asked. I said, "No."

"Too bad," he replied, "because we're looking for some to beat up." I realized that my companion was in fact Jewish. I was very much aware of Hitler's concentration camps and his policy of exterminating the Jews. I could not understand that these children who bought war saving stamps and whose parents were buying victory bonds to fight against Hitler had in fact a common enemy, the Jews. I was puzzled.

Ever since leaving Scotland I had corresponded with Stewart Black, one of the students at Dollar Academy in Scotland who had become a special friend. We had decided to form a club which we called the Good Friends League. Stewart printed up special stationary for us. Our small network consisted mostly of Dollar students, one of whom lived in Ceylon where his father was with the British forces. I broached the idea of forming a Toronto chapter with Billy, one of my new friends. He confided that "good friendship" would sound a bit flaky but if I wanted to organize a gang to beat up on other gangs in the area, every street seemed to have at least one, there would be no shortage of volunteers.

By the end of March, Father had completed his course as a machinist at Central Tech and was ready for employment. Bata wasn't quite ready for him and so he found employment with the John Inglis company, again on night shift. It was a dreadful job under very filthy conditions. I had never seen my father so dirty, not even after walking a whole day behind a set of harrows on the farm. Although theoretically he was well acquainted with the work of a machinist, actually running a machine was quite another thing. He suffered from a motor control problem, something that later also manifested itself in his operation of a motorcar. Father was extremely tense at work and once again came down with a rheumatic condition. It seemed that the machinist trade was closed to him. At that point the Bata option came alive. What they needed was a machine shop inspector. Father, with his mathematical ability and his exactness, fit the bill. Thus he left Toronto for the hamlet of Frankford six miles north of Trenton on the beautiful Trent River where the Bata works were located in an old paper mill. A new factory was in the process of being constructed.

Mother and I remained behind once again, waiting for Father to get established but also for the school year to end so that my education would not be interrupted once more. Occasionally Father returned to spend a weekend with us. He would tell us of his job and the beautiful area to which we would soon be moving. I was always sad to see him go and accompanied him to the bus terminal. We were consoled by the fact that he liked his job and that he was working with some Czechs, although that also presented some tensions. Of course we were also looking forward to the countryside which he had described to us.

At the end of June, I did in fact graduate from grade six. Father had hired a trucker to come and pick up our few possessions and take us to the new village of Batawa which the company was building to house its employees. As we left Toronto it began to rain and the driver put a tarp over the load under which I huddled. Mother sat between the two men in the cab. Miraculously the sun broke through as we turned off Highway 2 at Trenton and proceeded up Highway 33 along the Trent River. Through a hole in the canvas I took in the beautiful scene of hills and water. It reminded us somewhat of the Elbe River in our old homeland far away.

Our truck turned into the village of Batawa, past the new five-storey factory to the little wartime village and backed up to 33 Haig Street. Father awaited us on the porch of our brand new house. By this time I had great urgency for a bathroom and raced into the house. I almost forgot to use the facilities when I saw the beautiful, new, clean bowls and bathtub. I had never beheld such a wonderful bathroom, not even in our flat in Czechoslovakia. I fell in love with the place. I was even to have a room of my own. The packing box from Scotland was now up-ended to serve as my bookcase. Although our furniture was rather sparse we felt that we were finally at home.

The people of Batawa all worked at the same plant where shoe production had now taken a back seat to shell casings and other military equipment including aircraft parts. My father eventually became deputy chief quality control engineer. Mother became an employee in the shoe division. Life would now take on a more normal pattern.

Overseas the war raged on. Britain was under heavy air attack. Russia had been drawn into the conflict and the United States, after the Japanese attack at Pearl Harbour, also declared war on the Axis, as Germany, Italy and Japan became known. Mother, I know, had times of severe home-sickness, or at least a deep longing for the family she had left behind. There were times when the news in those early days of the war did not seem very positive. Hitler's forces were on the march, forcing Russia back almost to the Caucasus with its rich supply of oil. Rommel drove his tanks across the desert of North Africa towards Egypt. Scandinavia, except for Sweden which had remained neutral and where a good many Sudeten refugees were living, was under Nazi control. France had fallen. In the Pacific, Japan had island hopped and conquered much of Asia and China. The war that we thought would last no more than three years seemed anything but over. Canada sent its soldiers, airmen and sailors across a U-boat infested ocean while at home, industry churned out weapons and supplies in safety and without interruption. Canadians in general had no doubt about the eventual outcome, that we would win. Although we too were certain of the final outcome we had no illusions about how difficult or how long and costly it would prove to be.

Chapter Twelve

The War Years

Felix Skoutajan (far left) with fellow members
of the Czech Reserve Army

The War Years

After the final destruction of the Nazi tyranny,
they hope to see established a peace which will afford
to all nations the means of dwelling in safety
within their own boundaries.

The Atlantic Charter, 14 August 1941

Batawa was a wartime community built by the Bata Shoe
Company to accommodate the workers at their plant. The
village was quite unusual for that area. It was new, located
where, a few months before, there had been nothing but a
cow pasture. The houses were of a similar style, wartime
houses, they were called. In certain communities even now
fifty years later they can still be seen. Although the houses
were small, at that time coming from the rough log cabin in
the wilds of Saskatchewan we considered them almost luxurious. We lived on Haig Street named after the British
First World War general who had recklessly sent many
thousand Canadians to their deaths in the battlefields of
France. All the streets were unpaved and periodically the
township roadgrader would scrape through, lessening the
potholes and washboards. There were virtually no lawns
but only dirt beds which we raked level and some even

managed to coax a bit of grass to grow. A wooden board-walk crossed the ditch from the road and led to the front steps of each house.

There was a certain regularity to each day. The factory whistle summoned the war workers to the factory at seven o'clock. Half an hour later the whistle blew again to signal the work shift for the shoe employees. At eight fifteen in the morning, the children gathered at several places in the village to board the school bus, for which we had to pay, to take us to Frankford Public School. We were gone for the day, carrying our lunch boxes with us. This was considered quite unusual as most of the Frankford children went home at noon. At the end of the day the process was reversed. Again the factory whistle set the schedule. Many of us children awaited our parents at the plant gate and walked home with them.

Two Czech boys had acquired the very Canadian job of "paper boy" delivering the *Star* and the *Telegram*. These were rival newspapers and the rest of us children took sides according to the papers to which our parents subscribed. Ours was a *Star* family.

There was another significant division. The little community of Batawa was divided into two sections. Old Batawa had been established two years earlier to accommodate the Czech employees who had come with the company in the late summer of 1939, and New Batawa, where we lived, housed the others. Old Batawa was thus considered foreign territory by the Canadians and a bit of home for the Czechs.

What delighted me particularly about this community were the huge mounds of sand that were located at certain places along the roadside to be used for building purposes. They were our little world where my friends and I played. We built roads and tunnels on which we ran our little dinky toy vehicles.

My experience with sand went back many years to the sandbox behind our cottage in Czechoslovakia where my cousin and I played war games. He was older than I and had the privilege of being on the side of righteousness, Russia that was. I was inevitably the German aggressor who had to be bombed out of existence while he sang, *Und richten sie die Gewehre gegen die Soviet Union...* (And should they point their guns against the Soviet Union). With that a rock landed on the underground bunker where I had carefully hidden my head of state. That usually ended the conflict. I was not happy with my role or with war games in general. I preferred building roads and tunnels and even sometimes a castle.

Shortly after arriving at our farm in northern Saskatchewan I had another large pile of sand from the well that had been dug. My construction projects were undertaken once again. I made toy cars and trucks out of scraps of wood that I found around the farm. I was soon lost in this new world that took me far from the farm. Thus when I arrived in the community of Batawa I was pleased to find sand in which to recreate my imaginary world.

One day a rather significant event occurred on one of those mounds, one that made an important impact on me. I still remember it vividly. It was a Saturday morning when my best friend Teddy and I were playing on our favourite sand pile near his home. We were deeply involved in digging a tunnel, each from a different end with the intention of joining up somewhere in the depth of the pile within reach of our arms. We had noticed a man and a younger woman walking down the street stopping from time to time to talk to people. Presently they arrived at our little world. "Are you making rabbit holes?" he asked us.

I straightened up and looked at this stranger with surprise and annoyance. Rabbit holes, I remember thinking as I shook my head. I was filled with indignation, obviously this man had no idea that he was dealing with a veteran sandpile engineer. These holes were not rabbit warrens, they were sophisticated construction projects and I resented the stranger's suggestion. I can't say I disliked him and his companion, I simply felt they had no imagination. They were smallminded and that designation carried over to their mission.

Having made this negative contact he proceeded to invite us to a gathering of children that he was organizing down at the playing field. I had no idea what it was about. Teddy, being Canadian born and having come to Batawa from Bowmanville, a more traditional Ontario town, had some suspicion about this gathering. The man had evidently said something about the "gospel." I hadn't caught that reference. I think I had lost complete interest in the pair when they misunderstood our sophisticated purposes. Teddy shook his head, "He is a 'penny gospel' preacher, we won't have anything to do with them," he said. Teddy's parents were solid United Church, indeed, they were deeply involved in forming a Sunday school in one of the empty houses on our block. A Roman Catholic church was soon built and remains the only original building in the community of Batawa today.

Although the evangelist had maligned my engineering project I did go down to the playing field to see what was happening that afternoon. A small group of children had been gathered and the young woman who had accompanied our visitor was seated at a portable pedal organ. Teddy did not come with me. His parents had a car with some spare gasoline which at that time was rationed. They had gone to Trenton to shop. I was unimpressed by what I saw and heard and soon returned home. Nevertheless something had happened to me. I know it is unfair to have allowed this unfortunate encounter to colour an entire religious movement, but that's what happened. The stranger's kind of religion seemed trivial to me.

I believed myself to be a Christian and was quite offended when one day one of my more "Christian" playmates asked whether I had been "saved." I hadn't had an emotional experience as he suggested needs to happen as a stamp of the authenticity of my faith. I later discovered that I was what some theologians call "a culture Christian" as I didn't belong to any particular denomination. To be "unChristian" was to me a negative moral judgment. I considered my parents to be profoundly Christian, so much so they had to flee the wrath of fascism. To be a social democrat, that is to believe in equality, human rights and social responsibility was to me at that early age (fourteen) very much Christian.

Very soon after arriving in Canada my parents became members of the Co-operative Commonwealth Federation. That was alright in Saskatchewan but in eastern Ontario, there were few who espoused our political views and would have been horrified by my religious and political analysis. Teddy's parents were Liberals, while (another friend) Douglas' parents were Conservatives. I learned this as we dug in the sand pile together. It didn't seem to cause a barrier.

Although we spoke German, few in that community turned their back on us. I believe we were well liked. Father worked in the war plant, producing weapons to be used against Hitler. Mother worked in the shoe factory painting shoe soles. However, among the Czechs there was some ambivalence about us. We were Sudetens and after all the Sudetens were responsible for the breakup of the country in 1938, or so they believed. They found the distinction between "good" Germans and "bad" Germans somewhat difficult to grasp. German was German, but our family seemed to throw a spanner into that simple equation. Besides Canadian children, I had also come to know many of the Czech young people although most of them lived in the older part of this little community. I experienced a bit of coldness at the beginning but all that would soon change.

One evening, it was 28 October, the national holiday of Czechoslovakia, Vojta Beneš came to be the guest speaker at a celebration in Batawa. Vojta was the brother of Eduard, the president of the Czech government in exile in London. He was a professor at the University of Chicago. My parents had joined the Czech National Alliance in Canada, we had after all Czech passports and considered ourselves citizens of that country. The three of us went to the celebration which was being held in the factory cafeteria. As I recall we felt somewhat ill at ease. Although my parents could read and understand Czech, they could not speak it very well. The proceedings were entirely in Czech. Vojta gave an impassioned speech about the future of our homeland. At that time we still considered returning after the war was over and things were "normal" again. At least Mother had that intention while Father was somewhat more skeptical.

At the end of the meeting the national anthem was sung. I also knew it in Czech and joined in the singing. There were some curious sideward glances from some of the Czechs when they heard us singing *Kde domuv můj* with great conviction. At the conclusion Father made his way through the crowd of people who had gathered around Beneš. All of them knew Father and liked him personally, but they had these uncertain gut feelings about us. As Father approached him, Beneš recognized him and broke off his conversation and rushed to embrace him. Together they squeezed through the crowd toward Mother and I. Beneš and Wing Commander Ambrus, the leader of the Czech wing of the R.A.F., had visited us on our farm in Saskatchewan two years earlier. I recalled the time Beneš had noticed my dilapidated shoes and promptly loaded me into his car and drove to the general store where he bought a new pair of running shoes for me. He remembered us very well and immediately looked at my shoes and smiled. It was a warm hearted reunion.

I believe that Beneš may have guessed at our political circumstances vis a vis our Czech neighbours, for I heard him loudly proclaim, "Better a good German than a bad Czech." The explanation for that statement was that there were some Czechs and a goodly number of Slovaks who were collaborating with the Nazis, just as there were a good many Germans who stood firmly for a democratic and free Czechoslovakia and against Hitler; many of them were in concentration camps or abroad like ourselves.

I noticed the looks on the faces of our Czech friends that evening. Felix now was "Our Felix" although they were much surprised at this special encounter. At that time in Britain, Vojta's brother President Eduard Beneš had already made his decision that the Sudeten Germans would be expelled en masse from the country after the war, putting the German problem to rest for good. Of course he made exemptions for those Germans who had remained loyal to the country. He was angered and disappointed when Wenzel Jaksch, the leader of the Sudetens in exile, advocated that the Sudetens join the British army rather than the Czech battalion. Jaksch had gone to see the president in London to ask him about the rights of the Sudetens in a post war Czechoslovakia. When Beneš did not give a satisfactory assurance of accommodating the Sudetens' demands, Jaksch told him that he could not encourage Sudeten participation in the Czech army. Only a handful joined. Father, I know, felt that this soured the relationship and led to an even firmer resolve on the part of Eduard Beneš to "solve" the German problem once and for all. His brother Vojta disagreed and there were bad feelings between them on this matter.

All able-bodied men at Batawa joined the reserve army, now militia. Batawa had its own contingent, a company in fact. They drilled on certain nights of the week much to the amusement of us children who often attacked the 'platoon' with mud balls from behind some packing crates. Of course, Thomas Bata was the commanding officer. One of the platoons was made up of Czechs and was so identified by the shoulder flash "Czechoslovakia" rather than "Canada" although English was spoken. Father made the conscious decision to be in the Czechoslovak platoon and I have a picture of him in full battle dress displaying this shoulder flash as he set out for summer "war games" at the Connaught ranges near Ottawa. There his greatest thrill was blanketing out a small Ottawa valley community in a dense smoke screen. Although Father was certainly no militarist he had a good time with the men, especially now that he had Vojta Beneš' imprimatur.

Each Sunday in winter a whole column of us children set out across the field on our skis. Not far from the village there was an excellent ski hill which was much frequented. Of course there was no ski tow or any other convenience that are now everyday equipment for skiers. We herringboned up the hill and then skied down a distance of about a kilometre.

One morning as we proceeded to the hill Teddy, who was just ahead of me, announced, "Well, this is the last time we will be doing this." I was rather shocked and asked why. "They're starting a Sunday school and next week we will all be going there." I was indignant, first rabbit warrens and now religious interference in our activities.

"I'm not going," I announced and next Sunday found myself skiing alone, which wasn't much fun. The following Sunday I decided to follow my friends to the Sunday school at the recreation hall. I knew everyone there and was welcomed by Teddy's mother who taught and organized the

Sunday school. I didn't find it very exciting although I liked some of the music.

One day Mother decided to see what sort of Sunday programme I was involved in and came with me to the hall. On that occasion the regular pianist was missing and Mother was asked whether she could play. She was an excellent sight reader and happily consented although she did not know any of the music. She was immediately invited to come back next week to which she gladly agreed. It was the beginning of a new career for her.

Some months later, the teachers of the Sunday school decided that we should have an occasional service. They contacted the Board of Home Missions of the United Church who sent one of the ministers from Toronto's Church of All Nations. They wisely decided that inasmuch as Batawa had a substantial Czech population a minister fluent in Czech would be ideal. That minister turned out to be the Reverend Henry Vaclavik. He quickly established contact with the Czech people and began holding services in both languages once every month. They were held right after the Sunday school and I attended faithfully every Sunday. Father had met Vaclavik when he first came to Toronto and found him to be a well informed person. This meant that he appreciated that the political situation in Europe wasn't merely a war between the Germans and the Allies, but that there was an important ideological element underlying it all. This was something for which Canadians, at least the ones we got to know, had little appreciation. Henry Vaclavik also understood the tensions between Czechs and Germans. He brought out some of this in his sermons which tended to be very long because they were in both languages. I was never forced to go to church but generally found it more interesting than Sunday school. Vaclavik came more often and was always a welcome guest at our home.

His English sermons interested me greatly. This religion that he proclaimed was not trivial, not about rabbit holes, but about a world that was in turmoil with people caught in the maelstrom.

However I did like one of my Sunday school teachers, Gordon Ireland, who lived just around the corner from our place. I often went over to him when I saw him working in the garden and engaged him in conversation about religious matters. I do remember one incident that may shed some light on my thinking at the time. Ireland asked our class, all boys, who our idols were. I mentioned the name Roy Chapman Andrews which was unfamiliar to him. He inquired whether he was a flyer or soldier. He was neither, he was the curator of the Museum of Natural History in New York. All the other boys had chosen either war or sports heroes as their idols. I was very interested in nature and the first time I was in New York I visited his museum and was not disappointed. I think I might have become a naturalist, but one day after my confirmation Henry Vaclavik approached me and asked me point-blank whether I had ever given the ministry a thought. I replied in the affirmative. Indeed, a long time ago I had been fascinated by religion, even before I had come to Canada, but more than that Vaclavik had opened for me an understanding of the Christian faith that was much different from the fundamentalism and highly personalistic faith that was standard in that area of eastern Ontario.

My concern was whether I would be able to manage academically. I did fairly well in school but only with very hard work. I was a slow reader but a good writer. I had difficulties with math and although I was very interested in science, I found memorizing an agonizing process. Today I would be classed as somewhat learning disabled and given some help with my problem but not in those days. Nevertheless, I usually managed to be in the top three or four of my grade.

Batawa United Church flourished. We met regularly in the recreation hall. My mother usually played the piano, hymns that were totally strange to her. She did a good job adding a waltz rhythm to the music which seemed to appeal to everyone. Father also became active. When he first came to a service to check up on the Sunday activities of his son and wife some of his friends asked him, "Felix, are you baptized and confirmed?" Father explained that he had been baptized and confirmed in the Lutheran church, to which they enthusiastically responded, "Well then you can become an elder," and so he did. The church was very important in that community and provided a base for Czech and Canadian co-operation. My parents and I became deeply involved in that congregation and Father went on to become active at all levels of the United Church serving several years as commissioner to General Council, the denomination's top governing body.

After the war, Vaclavik stopped coming to Batawa and we were joined with the Frankford Pastoral Charge, a grouping of three rural congregations and one village church. Our new minister ,although a university graduate, did not have nearly the depth of theological or political sophistication that Vaclavik had shown.

The Frankford church with which we were linked had a youth group, indeed there were two groups with a younger one under the wings of the older group. It was a very active Young Peoples Union, as it was then called. Not living in Frankford but two miles away at Batawa I could not be as involved as I would have liked. I did know one of the girls in the club and one day discovered her very preoccupied with a project. When I asked her what she was worrying about she told me she was involved in a service at the church which would be led by the young people and she was to give the sermon. I don't know what possessed me to

189

sneer at this task, probably because it was diverting her attention from me.

"Well, if you think it's so easy, why don't you do it?" she challenged and for some reason, probably because I had already expressed my interest in the ministry, I accepted the challenge. A few weeks later, I preached my first sermon at Frankford United Church to a packed auditorium. But I am getting ahead of the sequence of my story.

Shortly after school closed for the summer all children above the age of fourteen lined up at the employment office of the Bata Shoe Company. I was very fortunate on my first try to get into the engineering department and spent the summer working on a horizontal grinder preparing the wheels on which the gun turrets of Lancaster bombers revolved. Although I had to work sixty hours a week, the pay was much better than those who worked on the conveyor belt in the shoe department. After the war I worked in the electrical maintenance department of the large plant.

The factory and the village were very much caught up in the war ethos. There were rallies and visits from government and military officials and as mentioned earlier, there was the reserve army which was trotted out at every special occasion. There was even a brass band which played a limited selection of regimental marches, *Colonel Bogey* seemed to be their favourite.

Many men and some women from the area joined the forces including the young man next door, only a few years older than I was. I remember him coming home in his uniform. One day, he returned proudly wearing navigator wings. When he left, it was for the last time; early in his career he was shot down and killed. He was an only child and his parents were deeply saddened. This incident raised a bit of a barrier between us and indicated that we were still seen as German, if not the enemy.

During the years of the war we had lost contact with

our relatives in Europe. One noon I managed to get to the post office before my father and discovered a rather strange letter postmarked the Red Cross in Geneva. I hurried home where Mother and I opened the letter. It contained the message that Robert, Father's brother, had been killed on the Russian front. Mother and I decided to hold on to the news until Father returned from work at the end of the day. He was shocked when we handed him the letter, but there was a sense of unreality about this message. We were too far away and the war created a wide chasm between us. Only one other letter reached us via the Red Cross in Switzerland. It brought us the news of the death of my father's mother.

With the end of the war, communication was re-established and the first letters arrived. There was relief. All of Mother's family had survived but two of Father's brothers had been killed, one early in the war and the other, Joseph the youngest, at the very end. But there was other news. The German people, who amounted to 85 percent of our home town, Aussig, were to be deported to Germany. This included all our relatives even though none of them had been Nazi; in fact, they had been active social democrats before the war. It was unbelievable for us. Of course this ended any hope that we would return. We made applications for Canadian citizenship and in 1947 were sworn in at a ceremony at the court house in Belleville. It seemed strange to us to have to kiss the Bible in that ceremony, nevertheless, we were proud to be Canadians.

CHAPTER THIRTEEN

Winners and Losers: 1945

Roman Catholic Church in Aussig
damaged in 1945 during bombing

Winners and Losers: 1945

*The Germans were always a foreign ulcer in our body...
we must begin to expell the Germans from our lands
at once, immediately, by all means, nothing
must be allowed to induce us to falter or hesitate....
Everyone must help in the cleansing of our homeland.*
President Eduard Beneš, Prague, 17 May 1945

The spring of 1945 was a memorable one, both for us here in Canada and for our relatives overseas. The war was drawing to an end. The armies of the allies were finally encroaching on German territory while nightly the cities were under heavy bombardment. Nevertheless, Germans were encouraged by their leaders to be brave; Hitler's scientists were in the last stages of the development of a "terrible and wonderful weapon" that would yet allow them to snatch victory out of the jaws of defeat. Fortunately, they lost the race for the development of a nuclear weapon.

The news in Canada was upbeat. Soon the "boys" would be coming home. Nevertheless the war plant at Batawa was going all out while we at school were often marched down to the basement auditorium to hear special radio programmes about the progress of the war. An old radio which stood in the middle of the stage was manned by the principal. It crackled and squeaked until the announcer's voice broke through with "This is London calling on the short-wave service of the BBC." We were excited not only to hear from overseas, but to miss one of our regular classes as well. Our school was quite small and all the students were gathered for these special event broadcasts, some of which were specifically prepared for schools. It was, of course, particularly important for those young people whose fathers or other members of their family were abroad.

The school I was attending was called a "continuation school." It consisted of two rooms on the top floor of the two-storey public school. Continuation schools were common at that time, particularly in rural areas. They consisted of four grades beyond grade eight but most children dropped out of school before that level was reached. Only those who intended to go to university enrolled in grade thirteen in one of the larger centres at either Trenton or Belleville.

I had a strange job in this school. I was the official time-keeper and bell ringer. On my first day of school in grade nine in September 1944 I happened to sit at the end of the row close to the door. The teacher arbitrarily picked me to become the bell ringer because of this proximity to the exit. It was a job that I kept for my entire four years at Frankford Continuation School. Both teachers, Mr. Sigsworth (the principal) and Mrs. Bennett, were new to the school as was all of the grade nine class. Mr. Sigsworth asked me to bring a watch to school and then provided me with a timetable of the classes. Because each room had two grades, the periods of instruction were short, twenty to thirty minutes, so the teacher could then turn to the other half of the class and work with them. At the end of each period the bell had to be rung. It was an electrical bell located out in the hall but the button for the bell was missing. Because of the wartime shortages of rubber there were no bell buttons available. I had to stick a pencil into the buttonhole to press the contacts together in order to cause the bell to ring. I thus became a clock watcher. As the minute hand moved toward the appointed time I got up and walked out the door, the only person in the class allowed to do so without special permission, and headed for the bell box. I was privileged and I admit that I sometimes abused it by making spares longer and unpleasant classes a bit shorter. The teachers were usually too busy to check the accuracy of my time-keeping.

I tell all this in order to explain what I did when, one day in May, the principal entered our room and announced that the radio had reported the war was over. Classes were dismissed for the day. I immediately got up and hurried to my bell. On the way I removed the forbidden chewing gum from my mouth and inserted it into the bell buttonhole until the bell rang. It continued ringing until the battery wore out; meanwhile my friends and I hurried home on our bicycles.

By the time we reached Batawa, a distance of about two miles from the school, the workers were also out in the yard, the factory whistle like my school bell had been activated. There was great excitement. The president of the company, Mr. Bata, was overseas but the general manager, Dr. C.K Hertz, spoke over the factory public address system. Everyone was excited and happy. Most people had friends or family in the forces and were relieved that fighting had finally ended.

Of course, the end of the war also signalled the end of war contracts for the engineering division of the factory. My father was in the aircraft division and soon heard of the cancellation of much of their production. For many the end of the war brought with it the question, what now? The war had ended the depression. Many remembered those difficult times and wondered whether they were going to return. But for the moment all was jubilation.

As Mother, Father and I gathered at the supper table that evening our thoughts and conversation were, of course, about the family we had left behind six years ago. Mother especially missed them. How soon would we hear from them and what would be the news?

The city of Aussig had remained untouched by the war until the final month. It was heavily industrialized and an important railway junction point. One night in February sounds of thunder could be heard from the north. A few hours later the sky lit up. News soon spread that the city of Dresden on the other side of the mountain chain was under heavy aircraft bombardment. Three days later my aunt Marianne arrived from that city at her sister's home in Aussig. She brought with her a tale of horror.

Marianne lived with her widowed father in the suburbs of Dresden. They both left the house when the bombardment began and ran through the streets. They just kept on running being joined on the way by everyone who could run. Streets were virtual rivers of people all seeking to escape from the flames and confusion. She was separated from her father who luckily got in with a group of older people being evacuated by trucks to the forests outside the city. Marianne kept on going along the Elbe River. She managed to get on a train a few days later that was heading south and ended up in Aussig on her sister's doorstep. When she and her father did return to Dresden and were reunited there was nothing there. The city centre was a pile of rubble. Even the suburbs were heavily damaged. Their house was no more. Everything was lost.

Aussig and environment had only experienced an occasional hit although some neighbouring industrial towns in the brown coal basin had been under heavy attack. The city was familiar with air raid sirens. Tuesday, 17 April, was a beautifully clear day. About 4:15 that afternoon, the sirens sounded. The electric clocks in the city all came to a halt at precisely 4:45. Bombs rained on the city destroying much of the centre core. The attack was most certainly directed at the railway triangle. A bomb landed right next to the town church blowing out all its windows and setting the church tower at the rakish angle which it has continued to maintain even to this day. From then on the city was subjected to continued bombardment as well as attacks by dive bombers who terrorized the civilians. There was a significant loss of life as men, women and children were caught under collapsing walls. Electricity and other utilities were destroyed. Three hundred and twenty-four houses were no more. The war had finally reached Aussig.

The city was prepared. Civilian work crews had constructed concrete tank traps in the main thoroughfares. Now the city became a place of refuge for people from the eastern front who were anxious to get out of the way of the Soviet army. Rumours abounded about the cruelty of the "Rutskys." They much preferred to fall into the hands of American or British troops.

On 2 May, the newspapers brought the report that the "Fuehrer" Adolf Hitler "fell in the faithful carrying out of his duties." Admiral Doenitz was now put in command. It was only months later that the truth was reported that Hitler had committed suicide in his bunker in Berlin. Day by day news reached the people of Aussig of the events marking the end of this era. Each citizen pondered the fate of this German city in what was once Czechoslovakia and would now be so again. Fighting was still raging in the mountains that had formed the border between Germany and Czechoslovakia, an area in which my parents and I used to ski. It seemed to be the last holdout of the German SS troops who had very little to lose and preferred to die with their boots on. All hoped that it would be the Americans who would be the first to arrive in the city. It wasn't to be so.

Russian and Czech troops, known as the Svoboda Guard, who had joined the allies toward the end of the war, took over the area. The government of the city was transferred into Czech hands. It was hoped by all that the city would be returned to its pre-1938 arrangement, a co-operation between Germans and Czechs. Aussig had been a model of good relations between the forty-five thousand Germans and the fifteen thousand Czechs. It was a hope doomed to disappointment.

In the night of 9 May, at about midnight, the radio reported the end of the war. Next day in the afternoon the first columns of Russian tanks entered the city from the north. Panic seized the people. Rumours of rape and plunder spread like wildfire. German people barricaded themselves in their homes. The following day citizens were called up to help remove the tank traps and also to begin to return the city to a viable community. While this work was in progress, long columns of soldiers, artillery and military vehicles entered the city, followed by prisoners and refugees. The city streets were blocked. There was great turmoil everywhere.

The fate of Aussig was to become *Ústí nad labem* (a Czech city). Street names and all other German language signs were to be changed. At first they were only glued over with Czech signs but soon the German signs were demolished to be replaced by signs with Czech only. Anything that reminded one of the city's German past was to disappear.

The population was intimidated. All Germans were ordered to wear white arm bands at least ten centimetres wide. Later, in some cities, those who could prove they had been active anti-fascists were to distinguish themselves with red armbands. But this process was often difficult. There were cases where fascists managed to pass themselves off as anti-fascists, but mostly it was anti-fascists unable to prove or convince authorities they had indeed been what they claimed to be. Large numbers of the population were interned in a wretched typhus-infected camp on the outskirts of the city where they were mistreated and undernourished.

At the Potsdam Conference, the allies under the pressure of Russia agreed that German minorities in Poland, the border having been significantly moved toward the west into German territory, as well as Hungary and Czechoslovakia, would be transferred to Germany proper, but that this transference was to be carried out in a "humane" fashion. Although I have told only of my hometown Aussig, the situation was the same in the whole of the former Sudetenland. In fact all of eastern Europe was on the move.

Little was known of this suffering "back home" in Canada. The reports that reached us through the media only very occasionally pictured a little of the actual severity of the conditions that prevailed. However, one graphic report came to us by way of an article in the *Toronto Star* under the headline, "All Ages, 4 to 80, Starve in Czech Horror Camp" (Special Cable to the Star, by Eric Gedye, October 3, 1945). "In order to avoid deportation to the Reich," Gedye wrote, "Germans in Czechoslovakia must show not only that they had not joined the Nazi Party or had not assisted Hitler's war effort, but that they took an active part in the Czech resistance movement." Our hearts fell for we were sure our relatives would be unable to provide proof that they had blown up bridges or derailed trains. They were German and that alone seemed to be proof of guilt. To be German was to be Nazi, or so it seemed in the newly liberated republic.

"Even Jews returning from Hitler's ghettos and concentration camps are put to the old Jewish starvation rations and refused Czech citizenship if at the last census they gave their race as German because they spoke German not Czech," the *Star* columnist reported.

The rules seemed to change from district to district at the discretion of local committees. In Komotau, the committee accepted as anti-fascists six to seven thousand Germans out of twenty-nine thousand. These were to be distinguished from the others by wearing red arm bands and were privileged to get the same rations as Czechs. The others had to do with the hunger rations given to the Jews during the Hitler era.

In my home town, on the other hand, no such distinctions were made. Thus when an ammunitions dump blew up, hundreds of Germans regardless of their political background, were brutally killed and thrown into the Elbe River. We were aghast at the news and what this might mean for our family.

Gedye describes the methods employed by the Czech guards: "Blocks of streets are closed and all Germans in the area are ordered to pack suitcases with a maximum weight of fifty pounds. Other property must be abandoned–they had already handed over all jewelry and precious metals–and then they were marched to concentration camps where they were kept until deported."

The writer had visited those camps himself and reported that while they could not be compared to Belsen they were nevertheless "horror camps." He stated that no one was tortured or murdered there, however, even that is being disputed. "The inmates are crowded together in huts regardless of age and sex. They sleep in double-tiered wooden bunks each containing a sack of straw."

Gedye was approached by men and women who claimed to have been in the camp for five months without any stated reason. They pleaded with him for help. A kindhearted guard told him that he had a baby of his own at home and wondered whether something could be done for these sufferers. He doubted whether he could continue to work there.

One of the inmates showed Gedye his release certificate from a concentration camp where he had been interned by the Nazis as a communist. He then had to relive that experience, this time at the hands of his liberators.

The smell of the place was awful. "The most shocking sight was the babies," the article continued. "One woman sat with a medicine bottle full of mother's milk–there was no other milk in the camp–trying to moisten the lips of the baby lying in her arms. The two-month-old infant had a wizened monkey-like face with dark brown skin stretched taut over the bones and arms like match sticks." The baby's skin was covered with gaping sores. Babies were born under those conditions without medical assistance. Hardly a day went by without one or two dying, but none of the inmates had ever seen a Red Cross visitor.

Those who had managed to stay healthy lived in utter boredom. Some busied themselves trying to do repair jobs around the camp with the most primitive of tools. Inmates claimed there was no water supply for sanitary purposes.

Gedye closes: "I have no fear of being accused of sentimental tenderness for Nazis when I describe these camps as an outrage to humanity and the good name of the Czechoslovak nation. Neither their government nor the population at large can be aware of these horrors or they would be stopped tomorrow."

We were in disbelief at such reports but were grateful to Mr. Gedye and the *Star* for making this known to Canadian readers. Although the massacre of Aussig is known to be one of the worst cases of Czech revenge, there are many other examples of extreme brutality following upon the liberation of the country.

One such extreme incident occurred in Prerov, formerly Prerau. On the afternoon of 18 June 1945, a train arrived bringing 265 people returning home from Slovakia where they had been taken to work in the fall of 1944. However, for the 71 men ranging in age from 14 to 80, and 120 women and 74 children, this was indeed the end station. They were kept on the train till late afternoon. Twenty soldiers of the Svoboda Guard armed with submachine guns then marched them to a place in the countryside not far from the station where they all were simply mown down. Their bodies were plundered. Personal identification papers were burned and the bodies placed in a mass grave. The train which held their baggage was also looted.

This incident was documented by the local police and reported to the Ministry of the Interior in Prague but nothing was done about it because of the chaotic conditions that prevailed in the newly liberated country.

Brno, the capital of the province of Moravia, had a large minority of Sudeten Germans. On the evening of 30 May 1945, all German residents were ordered from their homes. They were gathered in a park where they spent the night. In the morning the crowd was divided into three groups. They were then forced to surrender whatever money, jewelry, even wedding rings and bankbooks they had in their possession. The soldiers plundered them, taking their cases and bags. The order was given that anyone caught hiding anything would be shot on the spot.

This motley crowd of six thousand was then marched off in the direction of Austria. In the afternoon a vicious storm broke out filling the ditches and turning the road into a slippery mess. Those unable to carry on were taken to a camp where they were mistreated, raped and made to sleep on the bare ground or concrete. Many hundreds died of exhaustion; others were simply beaten to death.

July 30, 1945 is a day that is well remembered by many in what used to be the city of Aussig. It was a beautiful clear day but there was something in the air that was worrisome.

Could this be only in retrospect? At three thirty in the afternoon, the city was shaken by a mighty explosion that shattered windows throughout the city. Soon a mushroomlike cloud rose over Aussig. The first explosion was followed by a series of smaller blasts. It came from a munitions warehouse on the banks of the Elbe River. Prisoners from the camp at Lerchenfeld worked there sorting war items. Strangely, early that afternoon the prisoners, all Germans, were removed from this munitions dump leaving only the Czech guards. Someone reported seeing a single aircraft fly over the old factory. All sorts of stories were circulated by the people of the city.

The day before the explosion the much feared Svoboda Guards returned to the city. These were members of a special unit of the Czech army who had a reputation for brutality. Also reported was the arrival of a train from Prague that morning. Some three hundred male passengers between the ages of eighteen and thirty got off the train. Observers of their arrival described these men as "unsavory." It seemed that they had come from some penal institution.

No sooner had the sound of explosions ended when violence broke out in the streets. Men with all sorts of weapons, brick bats, iron rods, but also pistols attacked anyone wearing a white arm band. They were beaten senseless and dragged to the marketplace where a large water reservoir had been built for the purpose of firefighting in case of an air attack. The bodies were dumped into this container and those who still managed to surface were pushed under. By the end of the day there was no water but only bodies filling this large concrete cistern.

The worst of the violence took place at the river. When the soap factory on the Schreckenstein side of the river closed for the day the German workers were searched for weapons and then allowed to go home. Most of them had to cross the river but as they approached the bridge they were confronted by another checkpoint, once past they found that they could not turn back but had to walk into a waiting mob who attacked them. Many were thrown into the river and shot at if they managed to surface.

There was also activity at the other bridge where it was reported that a woman pushing a baby carriage was attacked and thrown into the river. The city was in an uproar. Germans went into hiding.

That afternoon my aunt Friedl, who worked as a secretary, was sent out by her boss to get a newspaper. On the street she met her father who was terribly upset and urged her to go into hiding. They tore off their arm bands and ran to the factory where he was working and hid until later that evening when a friend of theirs, a Czech, escorted them home. A curfew was declared, six p.m. for the Germans and eight p.m. for everyone else. Efforts were made by the authorities to restore order, however by that time over eight hundred people had been killed in a variety of ways. Rumours were circulating that plans were being made to evacuate all Germans from Aussig and surrounding area, to be sent into the interior to do forced labour. This did not happen but people lived in expectation of the worst.

It was conjectured that the explosion was the work of the "Werewolves," a gang of Nazi saboteurs that was on the loose and all Germans were made the objects of retaliation. On the other hand, it was suspected that the explosion at the munitions dump was set by Czechs themselves in order to justify a massacre. Suspicious events such as the arrival of the train of hoodlums as well as the Svoboda Guards and the instant response after the explosion give some credence to this suspicion. The incident was never solved but it left a legacy of fear and hatred. Interesting is the fact that no one remembers seeing local Czechs taking part, and there are many stories of Czechs aiding the wounded, taking them to hospitals or even hiding them in their homes. The Czech mayor of the city, Vondra tried to intervene in the massacre and almost became a victim himself. Nor were distinctions made between those who wore white arm bands and those who wore red arm bands. "German is German" was the rationale for this violence. Some feel that the anti-fascists were singled out for the worst treatment.

Few Germans were allowed to continue to live in their homes. The city was sectioned off and the houses were searched for weapons and German soldiers. Often the people were given only a few minutes to pack a few things and get out. At first great numbers were simply herded together and marched north into the hills and across the border into Germany. There they had to fend for themselves, begging until some relief was organized. Germany itself was in utter turmoil. There was great shortage of food and accommodation. Many of the elderly died on the march; others, in desperation, committed suicide.

Known Nazis were imprisoned in the former air force camp at Lerchenfeld on the outskirts of the city. This place was no better than the infamous Nazi concentration camps. Anyone caught trying to escape was executed. If a prisoner did escape, ten prisoners were shot in retaliation. The prisoners were used as slave labour with very poor food and no hygiene with the result that epidemics of typhus broke out from time to time and claimed its victims.

In the city, Germans were intimidated in many ways. They had to step off the sidewalk when a Czech approached and often times they were beaten if it was thought they didn't do it quickly enough. Germans were allowed to shop only at the end of the day when there was often little or nothing left. Few people had to worry about weight problems. There were always long line-ups and frequently the store closed long before the last customer got near the door.

Lotte, another aunt of mine, and her small son Frank

had a sister and father in nearby Dresden in Germany. She managed to get a spot on a river barge which had been chartered by a communist organization that was trying to get their people out of the country. She was not a communist but had some friends who were. It was September when she embarked on the crowded boat which took them down the Elbe River. There was no food provided. Everyone was expected to bring whatever provisions they could. They did not know the destination of the trip, except that it was going to Germany. People slept propped against a box or a wall. They washed in the water drawn up by buckets from the river. Lice and other vermin were a particular problem. After five days of travel the barge arrived at a camp near Wittenberg where they were disembarked and taken to old military huts.

The plans were to have virtually all Germans "cleansed" from the Sudetenland. Except for those who were driven out on foot or who ran away, this process was slow inasmuch as the occupation armies in Germany prevented it from happening until accommodation could be provided. This resulted in the grim events at the Czech and Austrian border where thousands were marched and simply dumped in no man's land. By early the next year, 1946, most Germans had been expelled except for those who were able to prove they had been anti-fascist saboteurs.

Friedl, whose partner was dragged off to a Nazi concentration camp where he simply disappeared before they could marry, was one of those given special privileges. She could have stayed in Czechoslovakia. However, her parents were expelled and she and her small son decided they would also leave. After packing up most of what she had, they were loaded into a cattle car for a West German destination. The train was at the German border very quickly but from then on the trip was slow and they did not know their destination. Occasionally the train stopped out in the country giving the passengers a chance to get off and do their toiletry. This was also precarious inasmuch as no one knew when the train would start again. Several passengers were left behind that way. There were some food stops where the American army had set up canteens; mostly soup and bread were dished out. After eight days on the rails they finally arrived at a displaced persons camp as these places were now called. In Friedl's case it was a schoolhouse where the classrooms had been turned into dormitories.

Literally millions of people were on the move in those early months after the war. It seems miraculous that some sense of order was ever restored, that relatives established contact again. In our case, it was our address in Canada that served as a connecting point.

One of the first letters my father received was from an old friend in a displaced persons camp in Germany. It read as follows:

"It is now six years, dear Felix, since we bade each other farewell in front of the Volkshaus. Our friends are scattered to the four winds in pursuit of their fate. Many have not returned. For some a simple turf covers their final resting place. Their bodies rest in the cold steppes of Russia, under the torrid sun of North Africa, in the high arctic of Norway, under the rough waters of the ocean. They unwillingly had to sacrifice their lives for a madman who brought chaos not only to Germany but all of Europe. This coward escaped the consequences of his actions in his Berlin bunker. I think of our martyrs, tortured to death in the concentration camps, thousands of our comrades, and those who managed to escape into exile." He goes on to describe his own fate and those of some of his and my father's friends. It is a bitter tale, especially as he decries the injustices of the exile and the end of the hope for a democratic, multinational community. Truly it was the end of a dream.

Jews were double victims of the Nazi era and its aftermath. In the 1921 census in Czechoslovakia, one hundred and twenty-five thousand declared themselves to be Jews. Of these, forty thousand claimed German as their mother tongue. According to the decree passed on 6 May 1945 all persons claiming German or Hungarian nationality were branded as untrustworthy. That some were of the Jewish race was not taken into consideration. Thus German Jews who had lived in the Sudetenland and survived the Holocaust were subjected to the same treatment as other Germans upon returning home. They were immediately put on the wartime food rations and deprived of any valuable possessions, particularly real estate. It must have been doubly degrading to these survivors to be forced to wear the armband that identified them with the very people who had been their enemy. Some were even interned in camps and later expelled to Germany. The anti-fascist social democrats declared their solidarity with these German Jews.

Such stories can be heard from any of the survivors of the ethnic cleansing of that terrible time. They are not to be considered as isolated incidents perpetrated by overzealous soldiers. President Beneš himself can be held responsible for not only the decrees that he issued but also the call he made for the "total elimination" of the Sudetens. An institute in the city of Munich has gathered and documented all the atrocities of that time.

We who lived in the comfort and safety of Canada were shocked by such reports and deeply concerned about the fate of our relatives "back home." We could not fathom the fact of the internment and deportation of people whose only crime was being German. Doubtless many of them had stood on the streets of Aussig and many of the other communities in the Sudetenland in the fall of 1938 when the German army arrived from across the mountain and cheered their arrival. Nevertheless the crimes that were now being perpetrated in the name of the liberated Czechoslovakia cannot be justified. We also asked ourselves what our fate would have been had we stayed behind. Undoubtedly Father would have been put in a concentration camp by the Nazis but even that would not have protected us from the horrors of which we had read. We attempted to write letters to our family as soon as mail services permitted. The first letter from Aussig, or Ústí nad labem as it was now called arrived in August with both good and bad news. Whether out of fear or for some other reason the letters did not convey the severity of the situation because the writers did not quite know of their own fate except that sooner or later virtually all Germans would be deported. With the co-operation of the Czech Social Democrats, the German Social Democrats were able to set up support, protection and negotiation for more generous deportation terms. A quarter of a freight car was allocated to each family. Thus my mother's family was able to take with them many of their possessions including some items we had left behind. It was interesting to notice familiar objects in the home of my aunt and uncle which used to belong to us, when I visited them ten years later. On my cousin's book shelf I am able even now to point out books that came from my father's library.

The nature of the injustice of the deportation of three million Germans from Czechoslovakia is still under active discussion between representatives of both nations. Václav Havel, upon becoming President of Czechoslovakia after the Velvet Revolution, expressed his sorrow over that chapter of history. However, the Czech government has offered no official apology. Financial restitution is not being considered. The expatriate groups are demanding from the Czech government an official withdrawal of the Beneš Decrees, those ordinances by the former president of the republic that all Germans were to be expelled and

Czechoslovakia become a truly uni-national state. This the Czech government has refused to do; as a matter of fact in a poll taken in 1996 an overwhelming majority of Czechs expressed their conviction that the deportation was justified by the events of 1938.

In 1996 when the former citizens of Aussig now resident in Germany wanted to set up a memorial to Leopold Poelzl, the last German Social Democrat mayor of their city, they were refused by the local Czech authorities. The memorial was then erected on Aussig Square in Munich where many of the expatriates now live. However, in 1998 a memorial plaque in Poelzl's memory bearing a picture of him has been located on the wall of the city hall.

Certain German deputies have threatened to make future entry of the Czech Republic into the European Union difficult if some resolution to the Sudeten situation is not forthcoming. In the meantime those who were directly affected by those events are becoming fewer. Soon the name "Sudetenland" perhaps even "Boehmen" (Bohemia) will slip into history to be remembered only by students of this turbulent century.

Those of us in Canada felt helpless in the face of the news that came across the ocean. For a time we did not want to believe it and insisted that it was only the militant Nazis who were being expelled. By Christmas 1945, the truth was out that many of our relatives and friends were celebrating Christmas under the worst conditions as deportees far from home or in the knowledge that this would be the last Christmas in their home. Many of us sent CARE packages regularly in the hope that some of them would find their way to our people in dire need.

CHAPTER FOURTEEN

A Visit

Grandmother Mahner in Canada, 1949

A Visit

Thrice happy they, and more, whom an unbroken bond
unites and whom love, unsevered by bitter quarrels,
shall not release until the last day of all.

Horace: Book of Odes

It was pitch dark as we pulled out of the driveway on our
way to the railway station. It wasn't a long drive, less than
half an hour. The Canadian Pacific Railway station in
Trenton, Ontario, is on the east side of the river in the
industrial area of the town. By the time we reached the station there was a hint of dawn on the eastern horizon. We
were early and the station was deserted. A green light
glowed from the station master's window that looks out on
the tracks. The staccato click of the telegraph could be
heard from inside. A couple of other cars were parked on
the cinder parking lot and another came along shortly after
us, probably belonging to the train crew that changed here.
The train we were awaiting was not a scheduled run but
what was known as a "boat train," a special train carrying
passengers to Toronto from a transoceanic liner docked in
Montreal and Quebec. It was unlikely that anyone other
than my grandmother would be destined for this station.

We walked up and down the worn wooden platform. All
of us were somewhat excited. We hadn't seen "Oma" for

almost ten years and much had happened since that time. Oma is my mother's mother, a widow of many years whose mission in life was to hold the family together. We had thwarted her efforts when in the fall of 1938 we fled from the Nazi takeover of the Sudetenland. Oma had tried to lure us back but the risk was too great for us and we left. She remained with the rest of her family and experienced the war and its terrible aftermath. Although a Czech and entitled to remain, she opted to go into exile with her son and daughter and their families. It was a difficult choice for one who had lived all her life in Aussig and environs.

The exiled families had settled in a small community near Frankfurt on the Main in what was then West Germany. Now in her late sixties, my grandmother undertook the long journey across the ocean to Canada. Was it once more to lure us back, to get her family reunited? We were suspicious.

Presently we heard the train's whistle in the distance. Soon its bright headlight rounded the curve and shone along the track to the station. The immense locomotive, hissing steam and power, pulled its long line of coaches past the station building. I was on the lookout for the conductor who would be standing on the step from which the passengers would be dismounting. That coach pulled past me and just behind the conductor stood my grandmother, a little old lady with her hair in a kerchief tied under her chin in peasant fashion as she had always done. I ran along beside the train till it came to a halt. Each window of the coaches framed several faces peering curiously into the dawn. Each head was that of a person with a hard history of war, refugee camps and losses of all sorts, now anticipating a new life in a strange country.

I would be experiencing many such arrivals in a few years time when during the summer months I was assigned to assist the United Church immigration chaplain at the ports of Quebec City and Montreal. Indeed, I would often meet *The Beaverbrae*, the very ship that had brought my grandmother to Canada.

The conductor jumped from the step as the train drew to a halt and placed his little foot stool beside the coach for the passengers to dismount. I was there in an instant to receive Oma in my arms. Mother and Father were hurrying up the platform to join me. Oma still smelled the same as I remembered, not a bad smell, just an Oma-smell that awoke many childhood memories in me. She had been my one and only babysitter when I was small. My grandfather had died many years before my birth. She had never remarried but dedicated herself totally to her family, a true matriarch.

Oma–her real name was Franziska although she was know as Fanni–was born in a small farming hamlet near Aussig. Orphaned as a pre-teen, her mother tongue was Czech but almost everybody in that area was able to speak some German. This was Austria after all, not the small country that we know today but the large Austro-Hungarian empire under the imperial Hapsburg monarchy, a multi-national state which after the First World War was broken up into countries such as Yugoslavia, Hungary and Czechoslovakia. Although German was the lingua franca, each ethnic group maintained their own linguistic and cultural identity.

In her teens, Oma got a job in a village pub as a barmaid. She was by nature a survivor who could live in the woods and off the land. She knew all about mushrooms, herbs and berries. Oma was a gleaner, going along the edge of the fields at harvest time to pick the leftover stalks of grain which she took home and ground in a coffee grinder to make flour. She knew how to roast barley in order to make a coffee substitute. She passed her skills on to her daughters. Her son was a good deal younger than his two sisters and did not quite inherit those skills. My mother also became a survivor, a skill that became very useful to us in those three years in the wilds of northern Saskatchewan.

While still in her teens, Oma met and married a railway worker who was German and could not speak Czech. I often wonder how they communicated; probably it was with love. My mother left me a portrait of her father. He was a good looking man with a large mustache. From my mother's stories, I conclude their home life was warm and close. Adolf, my grandfather, was a locomotive engineer. One day, as he was driving his engine slowly through the rail yard, he emerged from under a bridge to see a small child crossing the track. He yanked with all his might on the brake bar, bringing the train to a halt just centimetres from the child. But the brake bar had its revenge and snapped backwards catching Adolf across the chest. This accident precipitated tuberculosis and he died in his early forties.

My grandfather loved children. He was a storyteller and there was always a flock of neighbourhood children gathered around him. My mother and her sister Fanny worshipped him and his memory. I feel somewhat deprived not having known either of my grandfathers.

Oma lived by herself in the same flat in the centre of the city where she had raised her family until the expulsion of the Germans after the war. But each week she spent two days with her daughters doing a variety of tasks, cooking, baking, mending or cleaning. Fanny, the older daughter whose husband Max was also a railroader, went out to work and needed more help than my mother did. But Oma was my beloved grandmother and sitter.

Life in post-war Germany was difficult. The cities were destroyed. There were food shortages and so it was that my parents decided to make efforts to bring Oma over to Canada. That wasn't easy. Those living in displaced person camps had first priority for immigration. Nevertheless by the middle of the summer of 1948, arrangements were completed. Oma said her farewell to her family in Germany, moved briefly into the camp at Hanover and soon boarded *The Beaverbrae* of the Canadian Pacific Steamship Line. This ship was a freighter that had been rebuilt into a passenger carrying vessel. The cargo holds were divided into several floors of dormitories with double bunks. Over six hundred passengers were accommodated on one sailing from Bremerhaven to Montreal. It must have been a difficult trip but Oma never complained. She often talked about the babies on board who were accommodated in cardboard boxes to whom she devoted her attention.

We had a wonderful reunion on that railway platform. Oma turned to wave at her fellow passengers as the train moved off again. She had travelled with these people for almost two weeks. More than three weeks had passed since first encountering them at the camp in Germany. We loaded her heavy suitcases into the car. A wooden case was yet to come containing many items of interest, such as mother's old Singer sewing machine which Oma had taken with her from Czechoslovakia to Germany. She also brought pictures and bedding and table cloths and a lot of other things which evoked memories for us.

A private automobile was still an almost unheard of luxury in post-war Germany. Oma could scarcely believe we had a new car all to ourselves. The dawn had changed to morning as we drove from the station and pulled up to our small house in Batawa. I had turned over my room to Oma and was now to sleep on the couch in the living room. That was a bit of a sacrifice for me but I was pleased to have her with us. Although she had travelled all through the night and gotten no sleep, she began her many stories and accounts to bring us up to date with all that had happened since our 1938 departure. It was our first graphic description of the expulsion of the Sudetens and the changes that transformed Aussig from a German to a Czech city.

Batawa was a pleasant place for Oma. She began to attend the Roman Catholic church and met many of the Czechs who worked for the Bata Shoe Company. Shortly after arriving, she met Tomas Bata, the president of the world famous shoe company. She proudly showed him the shoes she was wearing and assured him that they were Bata shoes made in pre-war Czechoslovakia. Bata grinned and told her that his company could no longer afford to make shoes of that long lasting quality and remain in business.

It soon became apparent to her that her daughter, son-in-law and grandson had become Canadians, and could not be uprooted again. Oma became homesick and knitted socks to send to her German family into the toes of which she secreted little notes asking them to bring her back. We also became aware that the transplant was not taking and that Oma, while comfortable and in good health and putting on some weight (she was never a heavy person) was nevertheless unhappy. She was with us for two years almost to the day. Once more she boarded a freighter in Montreal and headed back across the Atlantic. We saw her off, not knowing whether we would ever meet again.

On my mission field placements in 1953, 1955 and 1956, as the summer employment for students for the ministry of the church was called, I encountered many displaced persons from Europe. I was fortunate to be assigned to work with the port chaplain on the St. Lawrence River. I was often reminded of my grandmother's arrival in Canada.

On some occasions I boarded the ships with the pilot at Pointe au Père near Rimouski, Quebec, to sail up the river and meet passengers en route. At that point the mighty St. Lawrence is so broad that one cannot see across. I would be taken out to the approaching ship on a tug and was often the first Canadian the passengers met. When it became known that I could speak German I was soon surrounded by curious immigrants with questions about work, accommodation and the cost of living. They would point to my shoes and other articles of clothing and ask how long one would have to work to pay for them; a practical way of discerning the cost of living in the new country that awaited them.

The trip up the river could take up to ten hours and I would be with the immigrants as we came in sight of land. Particularly exciting always was the arrival in Quebec City. The ship's railings would be crowded as they watched the citadel hill with the Chateau Frontenac high above the river coming into view.

It was from Dufferin Terrace, which runs in front of the Chateau, that I saw the first immigrant ship arriving. It was the summer of 1953 and Reverend Alex Murray, the chaplain, and I had come to meet the *Samaria*, the very ship that had brought me to Canada. I was excited as I saw the black and red funnel and the masts of the ship round the Island of Orleans and approach the city. We watched as it sailed on to Wolfe's Cove where the passenger terminal was located and then hurried to the docks to meet the passengers as they disembarked. All through the war, the *Samaria* had served as a troop ship; indeed, I have met some who had been transported by this same vessel.

The task of the chaplain was quite simple: meet people and do anything helpful for them, which often meant interpreting. Most immigrants spoke some German having been in labour and later displaced persons camps in Germany. However, Dr. Murray spoke five languages and was always in high demand. There were others assigned to port duty; including Louisa Mayova of the Women's Missionary Society, another Czech, who was also a linguist and great with children and old folks.

On my very first evening at the docks I met an elderly couple who were travelling to their son and family in Toronto. They had some difficulty finding their baggage, a very common occurrence which always reminded me of our own unfortunate experience many years earlier. After locating the missing trunk for them they were greatly relieved. They showed me a letter from their son in Toronto which was waiting for them at the ship's office. I saw that it also had a telephone number on it so I went to the phone booth in the customs shed and put through a call. The son came on the line and I asked him to hold until I brought his parents to the booth. The mother took the receiver to her ear but was almost unable to say anything. Tears streamed down her face as she listened to their son assure her that next morning he would meet them at Union Station in Toronto.

There were other times when I rode the boat train from Montreal to Toronto. I got no rest on those rides. At Oshawa, about half an hour before arrival in Toronto, the Reverend Horst Rueger, a United Church minister who had come to Canada from Berlin shortly after the end of the war, along with a group of German-speaking volunteers boarded the train and began passing out information sheets including warnings about shysters who would try to take advantage of the new arrivals by selling them insurance and a houseful of furniture on loans. They also encouraged anyone needing special assistance to remain on the train.

On arrival, I was able to witness the wonderful work done by the churches. Many who had no definite destination were taken to Howard Park United Church where a dormitory had been established and meals were prepared. The next day they were taken to the immigration and labour offices. This mission was very well organized and I was pleased to see what happened to the people whom I first encountered as they disembarked from their ship.

One of the other important tasks that we performed at the port was to copy the ship's manifest listing the passengers and their destinations. Where addresses were available, we sent notification to ministers informing them of the arrival. Many congregations followed through on this information and were able to welcome and help immigrants shortly after their arrival almost anywhere in Canada.

For three summers (1953, 1955 and 1956) I had the privilege of representing the church on the St. Lawrence River and later (1958 to 1960) at the ports of Halifax and Saint John. A whole book could be dedicated to the many experiences I had. It seemed that the events of my own life had prepared me for this type of ministry. It culminated in 1960, World Refugee Year, when I served as director for the programme of the United Church in sponsorship and settlement of displaced persons. It had been the hope of the United Nations to clear out all the camps in Europe and it was very successful. Some blind and otherwise disabled and sick were left behind to be looked after by agencies in Europe. However the forces that uprooted people were also actively producing ever more refugees all around the world.

I had no inkling that of any of this awaited me as I met my grandmother at the Trenton railway station that early morning. However, I shall not forget the faces of the immigrants in the train windows peering out into the dawn trying to get a glimpse of this new country into which they were being transplanted.

CHAPTER FIFTEEN

His Soul
Goes Marching On

Hanns Skoutajan helping new immigrants
arriving at the port of Quebec City, 1956

His Soul
Goes Marching On

Forgiveness is the key to action and freedom.
Hannah Arendt

The village of Bayerisch Eisenstein isn't much of a place. It seemed dark, shaded by the forest and the mountains that form the border between Germany and Czechoslovakia. As I approached the small community I saw a sign in English warning that I was entering the international border zone. At that time, 1957, there was something quite ominous about this border. The cold war was intense although there was as yet no Berlin Wall to divide the Germanies and symbolize the division of Communist East and Capitalist West, or Free World, as the West preferred to call itself.

I pulled my Volkswagen up to the railway station which appeared abandoned although a one car motor train visited the village twice a day. Tracks led up to the station from the west and beyond the station the rails had been roughly pulled up. I could see the rail bed continuing across a clearing to another village about a kilometre away. That village looked like a typical hamlet of the area. Smoke was rising from some chimneys, a sign of life. But between the station and that distant community there was a dividing line and a no man's land indicated by red and white stakes. A sign on the country road indicated a dead end. What I was looking at was Czechoslovakia, the land of my birth which I had left eighteen years earlier. It was the first time I had seen my homeland again, but I would not enter it for another decade. On this occasion I only stood and stared into the distance.

I recalled another occasion twenty years earlier when my parents and I went skiing in the mountains not far from Aussig and came upon those same red and white boundary stakes. I remember standing in amazement as I looked off toward Hitler's Germany. At that time, the Reich was the enemy and I regarded the distant country with a sense of foreboding. Now the tables were turned. What I looked at was communist territory almost equally foreboding.

The year 1956 was an exciting one for me. It was my last year at Queen's University in Kingston. I had worked slavishly hard to finish my degree with success. After convocation in June, I was ordained a minister of the United Church. I was fortunate to get a scholarship from the World Council of Churches to study Christian Social Ethics at the University of Muenster in West Germany. I spent the summer in my favourite city, Quebec, working as immigration chaplain on the St. Lawrence River, meeting immigrants from Europe. While there I received news that the German Academic Exchange had also given me a scholarship and so, on 18 September, I sailed as ship's chaplain on the MS *Seven Seas* from Montreal to Bremerhaven.

It was a long trip, eight days to Southampton, then on to Germany via France and Holland. The crossing of the English Channel was very rough but after leaving La Havre the sea had calmed considerably. Late that night I went out on deck to watch as we passed through the Straits of Dover. I saw lights on either shore. Beams from lighthouses winked reassuringly as we passed by. Once upon a time, not too long ago, this was dangerous no man's territory. The sea had been dark as pitch and U-boats lurked under the surface. I recalled the wartime radio drama, "Captain Midnight," that all of us children listened to with rapt attention as it dealt with espionage and escape across this very body of water. Now there was peace and I was travelling to the country that had been our enemy, from whose oppression we had fled. I was going to study theology, especially as it impacted on social responsibility.

Next morning we docked in Rotterdam, Holland, a country that Canadian soldiers had helped liberate. Most of the passengers disembarked here. Only very few of us travelled on to Bremerhaven where the *Seven Seas* would turn and take on a load of passengers, immigrants for Canada, most of whom had been displaced from Eastern Europe. They had been living in camps and were now seeking to make a fresh start in a new land, just as my parents and I had done in 1939.

Ten days after leaving Montreal, the *Seven Seas* approached the Columbus Quay, the modern transatlantic terminal at Bremerhaven. I disembarked, proudly presenting my Canadian passport as I went through immigration and customs conscious of the recent history of the land that I was entering.

As I prepared to take my baggage to the train that was pulled up at the terminal, suddenly there was my uncle Max whom I had not seen since that early morning when Mother and I had secretly slipped out of Aussig. He hadn't changed much, a little older certainly. His appearance did not betray all that had happened since we last saw each other, a war during which he drove trains bearing God-knows-what through darkened countrysides and bombed out cities. Then with the end of the war came those difficult times when they were expelled from their home to make a new beginning in West Germany, a country that lay in ruins.

Fortunately, being a locomotive engineer assured him of a job almost immediately in a land that was desperately short of employable and reliable male workers.

It was a very exciting reunion. Max had come to meet me and accompany me on the day long train trip to Steinheim am Main, a town just east of Frankfurt. We had lots of time to talk on this trip. He told me something about the war. I could see that many of the cities through which we passed even then, ten years after the war, still bore the marks of wartime devastation. Finally, after changing trains in the huge and sooty Frankfurt station, we arrived in Steinheim. A bus took us to the home of the Hanke family. The place was quite primitive from my Canadian perspective. It had only an outdoor toilet to accommodate all the people of the house.

Max let me into the house and took me to their second-storey flat where I was awaited by my aunt Fanny, who had been to me like a second mother, and of course my grandmother who had been with us for two years in Canada. Tears coursed down our faces as we embraced each other. It seemed like a miracle that we were all together again after so much turmoil and change.

The following day, Max took me to Hannau, a neighbouring city, to meet my cousin Gert who was a lawyer working for the tax department. In a moment it was as though we had never been separated. He has always been more like my older brother than a cousin. As a child I usually inherited his castoffs that were still too good to be thrown away. He too had experienced hardship and war but Gert is brilliant and had hoped to become a medical doctor. In the last year of the war he joined the German navy knowing that that branch of the military was port bound except for its submarine section. It continues to amaze me how selective the Nazi administration had been, as they tried to spare those who were obviously gifted. Gert was sent to work in a medical facility. Close to the end of the war he faked illness and switched x-rays with another patient. He barely escaped being operated on when the war ended. Then followed the perilous journey home to Aussig.

The last leg of that journey was done in a coal train hidden among the coal. Former German military personnel were in extreme danger on returning home. One night the train halted and Gert had the uncanny sense that he must be nearing home. He crawled out of the coal and indeed discovered that he was only a short distance from the house where his parents lived. By this time Aussig and the entire Sudetenland was in the midst of the turmoil resulting from the change from German to Czech. Germans, wearing their white arm bands, were mistreated and humiliated in many ways. Workers were needed in the coal mines and so Gert went to work in the pits. It was hard work in very unsanitary and unsafe conditions. He became very ill and had to stop working. Fortunately Max, his father, who spoke perfect Czech, continued to be employed as a locomotive engineer; they were in short supply. Finally the day came when they too had to pack up their possessions and leave their country.

In Germany Gert tried to go to the university but there was no room in the medical faculty. He was, however, able to find an opening in the faculty of law. At that time courses were shortened and Gert was able to complete his studies in record time. He had married and had one child, a son, Peter-Renee.

In the next few days I was reunited with a number of my other relatives from both sides of the family. I was particularly glad to meet Robert, a cousin on my father's side who spoke excellent English. His father had been killed in the early days of the war. Although my German was coming back very quickly now that I was in total immersion, it was nevertheless good to be able to express myself in what had become my first language.

Soon it was time to begin my studies in Muenster. This city in northwestern Germany had also been heavily bombed, the evidence was still visible. Mounds of rubble were everywhere. The Roman Catholic cathedral, a large Romanesque structure in the centre of the city, had been heavily damaged and was only reopened the very week I arrived in Muenster.

Along with my courses I undertook a volunteer job. It took me to a refugee camp on the outskirts of the city where I did little more than meet and converse with people who had been uprooted from Pomerania which was now part of Poland. Indeed, almost daily, trains were arriving in West Germany with Germans who had been expelled from those eastern regions of what used to be Germany. They arrived with their bundles of possessions. Many of them were elderly and often sick. It seemed like the whole continent was still on the move even now more than ten years after the war.

I was very fortunate to get a room at the Hamann Stift, the newly opened student residence of the Evangelical Church. Next to the residence was a thirteenth century chapel, the Johanniskirche, where every morning at seven forty-five the students gathered for worship. It was there that I became familiar with German hymns and liturgy. I was also called on to take my turn to lead in worship. There was something deeply spiritual in those meditative times that fed my soul as I struggled with the many political, social and theological issues I encountered.

As mentioned before, I had come to study Christian Social Ethics at the University of Muenster. The city is well known as the place where the Peace of Westfalia was signed ending the Thirty Years War. Much of the inner city was restored in the old style and was quite beautiful. The Lamberti Church, with its Wiederteufer cages which hung from the high tower of the church in which Anabaptists had been imprisoned to starve to death, reminded all of the turbulent and cruel history of Europe not only in this century but earlier.

Muenster is generally thought of as being Catholic, nevertheless the university had a small but excellent Protestant faculty. It had not been my first choice, I would have preferred Marburg or Tuebingen, places that had a reputation for theological studies. However, Muenster turned out to be an excellent place to study Christian social ethics as well as other areas of interest. Another very important advantage was the fact that there were very few foreign students at Muenster. One who became my very best friend was Alastair Stewart of Edinburgh who came to Muenster to study German literature. Al had been an active member of the Student Christian Movement and a member of the Presbyterian Church. He had a great sense of humour, spoke excellent German and was a wonderful resource person. Shortly after arriving in Muenster, Al made connection with the British forces stationed in the area and found someone who was able to get Nescafe for us cheaply. It was still expensive and hard to get in the regular stores in town. The coffee supplied by the residence each morning was a poor imitation of that beverage. We made a deal: I prepared the breakfast which meant going to the bakery to pick up fresh buns and I would have unlimited supply of good coffee. It worked out very well. He and I often discussed our minor grievances with the "Jerries" as Al liked to call them privately.

A great deal was happening in the fall of 1956. Hungary was undergoing revolution and the Middle East was in turmoil. It was the time of the Suez crisis. Students in Muenster were quite upset over British involvement in Egypt. I sensed a certain relief among them that Britain could also be seen as an aggressor rather than only

Germany. One evening I joined several thousand students in a silent protest march through the inner city. We were a long column of students walking through the semi-dark streets of Muenster. Nothing could be heard except the sound of shoes on the cobblestones. It was awesome. Following the march there were services of prayer for peace in both the Protestant and Roman Catholic churches.

The Evangelical Church (Lutheran/Reformed) was experiencing a crisis. The German army had been reconstituted and the government had approached the church to supply chaplains for this new *Bundeswehr* (Federal force). The church, particularly the Protestant church, was split on this issue. Those who had been part of the Confessing Church, that group which had split off from the state church in the Hitler era in faithfulness to God rather than state, were dead set against a German army let alone having the church supply chaplains. As one explained to me, if he had to counsel a soldier the only advice he as a Christian could give would be to get out of the military as quickly as possible. On the other hand there were many of the younger students who had had no experience with the struggle of the church during Nazi times. They saw only the model of the U.S. and Britain which they wanted to emulate. Al and I, as representatives of countries that had a military and a chaplaincy, were drawn into the debate though both of us were "mildly" pacifist.

The highlight of my fall semester was the weekly three hour seminar on War, Military Service and the Gospel. It was an interesting group which met from four until seven every Monday evening, made up of not only theological students but also students from other faculties such as law and journalism. I was asked to give a paper on the position of Reinhold Niebuhr, the well known American Christian leader and ethicist. Niebuhr had been a pacifist but later in the war came to believe that there was such a thing as a "just war." I found it very difficult not only from a language point of view but also because the subject matter troubled me. After giving my paper, I was attacked by all as if I were Niebuhr and had to defend myself. This was the usual procedure and it was vicious. I remember walking home in a daze after that interrogation. It did, however, help me to be a little less blasé about the victor's righteousness.

On returning to Canada I felt compelled to rethink the Christian perspective on those issues. I also came to appreciate Christian pacifism and the Social Gospel movement that had flourished before the war particularly at Queen's University under the leadership of Professors Estall and Vlastos. Mine was not only a theological problem, it also had personal overtones. I had to remember that my parents and their friends had been the victims of fascism. We were certainly against war but knew that Hitler had to be defeated. The chance for a bloodless overthrow of the Nazis had been missed in compromise and even collusion. Was the war therefore a necessary evil? My relatives had been expelled from their homeland after the war under the pressure of communists at the Potsdam conference in the summer of 1945. Who were my real allies? What is my political responsibility from a Christian perspective?

I recalled the return of the Hastings and Prince Edward Regiment from Europe in October 1945. All of Belleville and surroundings turned out to meet the troop train as it arrived at the station. It was preceded by a hospital train carrying the wounded, a powerful reminder of the cost of war. The local reserve army (militia) which included my father was there to welcome them and march with them from the station to the armories. I stood in the crowd with my school chums watching our fathers parade by. These were the victors. They had conquered Hitler who was a personal enemy of my people. But I was also aware that I was German speaking. I had only been in Canada six years. I

235

experienced that strange ambivalence once again. Nothing was cut and dried as it seemed to be for many of my friends, both Czech and Canadian. I still sense that feeling each Armistice Day when I join others at the cenotaph ceremonies.

The first line of the Czech national anthem "Where is my home, my fatherland..." poses a question that was very real for me. I expressed this longing in a hymn I wrote in the eighties when I was minister at St. James-Bond United Church in Toronto. I called it "Sanctuary." The suggested tune for this hymn is "Mannheim" by Friedrich Filitz:

Where is home, the land familiar,
Where the village known so well,
Where the mountain and the river,
Where the forest and the sea,
Where the city thronged with people?
Land of birth remember me.

Long the journey's search for freedom,
Hiding, running through the night,
Seeking refuge among strangers,
Begging help, a place to hide;
Strangers seeking safer havens,
Often hated, seldom loved.

Some there are, compassionate people,
Know their Master also fled,
From mad Herod's purge of children,
Waiting for the storm to pass.
Willingly they offer shelter,
Brothers, sisters, Christ our host.

In God's realm there are no boundaries,
No barbed wire, trenches, walls,

Where there are no racial ghettos,
All are welcome, none are lost.
Peace and justice is the charter,
Fear deported, love enthroned.

In the late spring of 1957, I met my mother as she made her first trip back to her family. She arrived at Bremerhaven just as I had, also on the same ship, the *Seven Seas*. I had acquired a Volkswagen and together we drove to Steinheim to our family. It was a most exciting reunion. One of the first things my mother did as she was surrounded by her sister, brother, mother and others, was to reach into her purse. She brought out a gold watch which had belonged to her father. Her brother Dolf had been in possession of this watch after their father had died. On the morning that Mother and I escaped from Aussig, Dolf had thrust this gold watch into my mother's hand, "Take it," he said, "perhaps you might be able to get some money for it if you are in difficulty." Mother had treasured this watch. It had gone with us into exile to Britain, to Canada and now was returning to its initial guardian. We stood in a tight circle embracing each other with tears streaming down our faces.

The graves of my grandfathers, none of whom I had ever met, remained in Czechoslovakia. Their final resting places have disappeared. I have scattered the ashes of my parents on a hill above the Trent Valley where they had felt so much at home. There is no marker for their graves. By now their ashes have mingled with the earth of this country Canada which they adopted and which accepted them. The ideology which motivated their lives, forcing them into exile, lives on even in a time when, under the pressure of globalization, a compassionate society is being relentlessly threatened by commercial pressures.

On a holiday trip to the Adirondack Mountains in

upper New York State, we came upon the memorial to John Brown who had been one of the saints of the anti-slavery movement. My parents and I stood before his statue and read the words of the famous hymn "John Brown's body lies a mouldrin' in the grave, his soul goes marching on." Father admitted that this was his concept of immortality. It was not some ethereal, disembodied entity floating in space. This was his statement of faith. I hope that I and my family embody not merely his genes but also his faith. I see some real evidence of that in Stephen and Karla, our children, who have both chosen idealistic professions. My prayer is that there will come a time in the not too distant future when people will dare to grasp the humanity that God has given us and live responsibly with one another. We dare to wait, albeit impatiently, for that occasion.

In the fall of 1957, I returned to Canada, again on the good ship *Seven Seas*. I boarded the ship at Southampton having taken some time to tour in Britain. I had been to Scotland to visit Dollarbeg and the Dollar Academy where we had stayed after fleeing Czechoslovakia. I had also visited the island of Iona on the west coast of Scotland, the place where St. Columba had set up his mission so long ago. It was now administered by the Iona Community, a group of Christians from Scotland and many other parts of the world including Canada.

The old abbey was a place for quiet meditation and I needed time to think about all I had learned and experienced in this last year. I was also looking forward to my new position as chaplain to students at Dalhousie University as well as immigration chaplain at the port of Halifax.

It was easy to make friends on the island, indeed, a storm came up that isolated us from the mainland for a few days. It quickly drew us together. The members of the Iona Community are well known for their Celtic spirituality as well as their social activism. They combined their faith and political outlook and gave me something of a model for my ministry to come.

After visits to Glasgow, Edinburgh and London, I boarded the boat train to Southampton where the ship had docked. It had come from Bremerhaven bound for Canada with over one thousand passengers. Shortly after leaving port I heard myself paged to report to the chief steward's office. I knew Herr Gruber well from my previous involvements with this immigrant ship. He looked at me seriously and then explained that, "as you know the immigration board of the Lutheran church in Hanover supplies us with chaplains for each of our trips. We also had a chaplain, however, we don't any more. Our pastor went for a walk in Southampton, lost his way and missed our departure. We have just received his radiogram from port."

Mr. Gruber paused and looked at me. "I suppose," I said, "that I am to take his place." He nodded his head affirmatively. It was going to be a busy trip for me.

There were to be chapel services every morning, basic English courses daily and for the rest of the day I was also to be available for chats and counselling. I had brought with me a slide presentation about Canada which I had given on a number of occasions in Germany. Mr. Gruber took me down to the baggage hold of the ship to find my steamer trunk where my slides and projector were located. On several evenings during the eight-day crossing, I gave this presentation again. The immigrants were most interested to find out more about the land to which they were travelling.

Sunday came in the middle of our trip. I organized an ecumenical service for all at which Captain Oltmann read the lesson. I was fortunate that two German exchange students from Muenster, Gert Winkhaus and Hans Riedl, were also on board and I recruited them to help me in my ministry. It was a busy crossing, not like the first one that brought me to Canada in 1939. Again I felt myself deeply enriched by the contact with the immigrants whose backgrounds were familiar to me. I could identify with their excitement and anticipation as we sailed up the St. Lawrence River to Montreal. They too had been uprooted and now awaited transplanting into Canadian soil.

CHAPTER SIXTEEN

Transplanted

Felix Skoutajan in Canada at age eighty-three

Transplanted

There is properly no history, only biography.
Ralph Waldo Emerson

Radomir Luža closes his study of *The Transfer of the Sudeten Germans* quoting Hans Krebs, a Sudeten German deputy before the People's Court on 15 January 1947:

"In this moment a full thousand years of common, hard, but also great historic periods are closing. The Czech Nation will now, at the last, live alone in its national State, which not only in name, but also in fact is really becoming a national State. Three million Germans have been transferred. This is the greatest transfer since the migration of nations.... Nearly one third of the population of Bohemia, Moravia and Silesia have left or are leaving their old homes. They are leaving behind their homes, what they once called their property, their past and their dead. They are leaving the work of millions and the work of many centuries, never to return. It is hard for anybody who has not gone through it to measure the moral and spiritual burden we are bearing now....From this time you will have no more nationality disputes in your country. I only wish that the great sacrifices we are making may not be without profit, but that from them there may at last be born a peaceful fellowship between us—which, alas, we did not succeed in establishing

Uprooted and Transplanted

in one State—namely, the fellowship of the German State
and the Czech State, which will again be neighbours in the
future....

"May the separation of Germans and Czechs finally
bring peace to both! May the suffering of our time end our
suffering for all time! Only so will these immeasurable sacrifices have any meaning which we Sudeten Germans must
now make and which the Czechs also have had to make in
so great a measure. They will have served the highest ideal
of mankind—a lasting and honourable peace."

Luža comments, "It is up to rising generations of both
nations to implement this profession of faith."

The Transfer of the Sudeten Germans is a thorough study of
Czech-German relations between 1933 and 1962. Luža's
judgments, however, are weighted in the Czechs' favour in
defending the Transfer and the Beneš Decrees. He blames
the Sudetens for the Munich Agreement, for providing Hitler
with the excuse to absorb the young republic. Indeed, Czechs
have much to be angry about—the years of the Protectorate
(1939 to 1945) were years of hardship even horror.

True, the majority of the Sudetens vigorously supported
Konrad Henlein's party, the Sudetendeutsche Partei, and
enthusiastically welcomed the mobile German army as it
made its way over the mountains to the Bohemian plains.
Dirndl (the traditional costume) clad women cheered and
threw themselves on their "liberators" while their men
joined the ranks of the SS and SA. It was an embarrassment
for those who held to a different ideology.

Unfortunately Luža doesn't take into account the thirty-five thousand anti-fascist Sudetens who were rounded
up and transported to concentration camps in the Reich and
those of us, another two thousand or more, who were successful in fleeing abroad.

Luža does make mention of "unfortunate excesses" after
the war on the part of Czech zealots and plain hoodlums

who took advantage of the unstable postwar situation. He documents the orderly transfer in "heated trains" to West Germany, and quotes American and Russian generals praising the smoothness of the transfer. Indeed, one must marvel that over three million people were "ethnically cleansed" from the newly liberated republic in a relatively short time. But about those "heated trains"?

Luža exonerates the Czech government and Beneš, the president, by referring to the Potsdam Conference of July 1945 in which the Allies assumed responsibility for this dislocation. These were, however, the very powers who had signed the Munich Agreement in 1938 or stood idly by to observe the Nazi rape.

In 1964, from the ivy-covered haven of an American University, Luža takes comfort in Krebs' words. Hard as it was he rests content that it was "all for the good, that justice was served and the future was secured."

Unfortunately a normal and neighbourly relationship between Germany and Czechoslovakia had to wait for another thirty years to pass until the Velvet Revolution had taken place and the Iron Curtain dividing Europe had collapsed in a heap of rust. That period of time was difficult for the citizens of Czechoslovakia and many a Sudeten in the West may have breathed freely, thankful that he/she did not have to endure the soul destroying communist interregnum.

The Sudetens did well in Germany. Many of them received compensation and pensions from the German government. They accepted responsible roles in their new homeland. Some such as Wenzel Jaksch and Volkmar Gabert became deeply involved in German as well as European politics. Entrepreneurs, professionals, tradesmen and trade unionists brought their skills with them. Germany's gain was Czechoslovakia's loss.

While the *Landsmanschaft* (conservative Sudeten nationalists) may rally from time to time, rehearsing old injustices and calling for compensation, few if given the opportunity would return. Certainly the sons and daughters of those expelled have become good citizens of Germany, Canada, the United States, Britain and Sweden.

Nevertheless, there is a strong sense that an injustice was committed. How long must a people reside in a land, how many generations must be buried beneath that turf before they can call it home? Obviously the Czechs looked upon these German speaking people as foreigners who did not belong in spite of almost eight hundred years of residency.

When Luža wrote his book, the term "ethnic cleansing" was hardly current. Yet it accurately describes what took place. It has become almost commonplace for a majority to summarily dismiss a difficult minority rather than admit that they have as much right as the others to be, and to be accepted as part of the whole.

I make no apologies for the fascist Germans of the Sudetenland. They behaved shabbily, they allowed themselves to become pawns in Hitler's aggressive push toward the East. But even without the Sudetens, Hitler was prepared to expand his empire to the Caucasian oil fields. His megalomania conjured a mighty Roman-like empire worthy of the Aryan heritage.

Could the postwar period have been different? Could Germans and Czechs have continued to live together in a co-operative federation? It's never smooth sailing. I think of my own country Canada where the French Quebecers are restless in the confederation and, in a referendum in the fall of 1996, came within only a few thousand votes of breaking from this union.

Soon after the demise of the communist world Slovakia separated from its Czech partnership. Tensions between the two are long-standing. Multi-nation states such as Yugoslavia are tearing themselves apart in bloody conflict.

The Czech/Slovak dissolution was without any hint of violence. In the meantime a European Union is developing to which every independent state wants to belong. Trade alliances such as the North American Free Trade Agreement, the power of the World Bank and the International Monetary Fund are forging new international relationships. Transnational corporations with assets greater than many nation states are becoming the global dictators.

Globalization is a reality. This world community is getting smaller all the time. Co-operation rather than domination is important in this global village. We humans must learn to get along and ethnic sensibilities must be respected.

Those democratic socialists who worked together in the old Hapsburg empire, struggling against imperial rule, had an important ideal that united them. They were internationalists who believed in the dignity of working people. They believed in democracy and social responsibility and would find little satisfaction with a corporate globalism. From time to time these ideals still raise their heads in a capitalistic world. Perhaps, hopefully, their hour will yet come in this worldwide community. Uprooted and transplanted, their ideals may flourish.

❊   ❊   ❊

The funeral service was drawing to a close. During the hymn the minister who happened to be me, came down from the chancel as the congregation sang the final hymn "Now thank we all our God." It was a mixed gathering of people, members of the congregation who had known my father and mother, as well as others from further away who were strangers in this house of God, but who had known Felix for many years. Some of them had fled and immigrated with him almost half a century ago. A goodly number of them had little or no connection with any church. These stood and held the hymn book reverently while listening to the words being sung.

As the hymn came to its conclusion the minister stood before the plain pine casket with its bouquet of red carnations and the picture of Felix on it. The last words were about to be spoken as the hymn ended.

"Felix Skoutajan, *der Herr segne Dich und behuete Dich*" (The Lord bless you and keep you). I remembered once again Felix at the farm gate in Mocra Lhota with tears on his cheeks announcing to Mother and me that it was all over, that everything was lost.

"*Der Herr lasse leuchten sein Angesicht ueber Dich und sei Dir gnaedig*" (The Lord make his face to shine upon you and be gracious unto you). I recalled that early spring day as our hay wagon creaked to a halt near a dilapidated log cabin that was to be our home in the wilderness of northern Saskatchewan.

"*Der Herr erhaebe sein Angesicht ueber Dich and gaebe Dir Frieden*" (The Lord lift up the light of his countenance upon you and give you peace). Frieden, Paix, Mir, Peace, beautiful words all, words that belonged to a scarce human condition that Father longed and hoped for and had striven to achieve.

The minister now turned and began his walk down the centre aisle to be followed by the casket. Softly the organ began the recessional as if from a distant trumpet. Soon those who were strangers to that church caught the melody and as the organ repeated the music they joined in to sing that old marching song of the Sudeten Social Democrats, "*Brueder zur Sonne, zur Freiheit, Brueder zum Licht empor*" (Brothers, onward to the sun of freedom). Now the organ swelled, no dirge this but a triumphal expression of a faith in the future of humanity. They fell in behind the casket and accompanied it to the church entrance. Only the minister followed it to the open doors of the waiting hearse. The casket slid into the big black car. I briefly touched the wood that would soon be consumed by flames. The door was closed, the car moved off.

End of an era. I remembered pictures of battles long ago when the soldiers lined up in formation, one line behind the other. Shots were fired. After the first volley, the dead and wounded were carried off, the empty places were quickly filled by those who had stood behind. I understood that now I was in the firing line.

CHAPTER SEVENTEEN

Rooted

Memorial sculpture for the victims at Dachau
by Nandor Glid

Rooted

Ad mare usque, ad mare
(From sea to sea)
Motto on Canada's coat of arms

On the last day of September of 1998, I boarded a plane in Munich to fly home from Germany. Twenty-five Canadians who, like myself, stem from the Sudeten area of the former Czechoslovakia had attended the day of remembrance of the Munich Agreement of 1938.

The plane took off in a northwesterly direction. For a time I was able to see the countryside below us, those neat little villages with their uniform red tiled roofs, churches and other buildings and the orderly laid out fields surrounding them. Occasionally an autobahn with its madly racing traffic coursed through the wooded hills below, a river snaked its way across the countryside. The plane ducked into the clouds and later emerged over the North Sea near the British coast. We crossed that island nation that had once been our refuge and then just beyond the Hebrides off the coast of Scotland the world was once more hidden from our view. For many hours the engines droned on in bright sunshine while we ate our lunch, drank, watched the movie, read the in-flight magazine or tried to sleep. My mind was absorbed by all that I had experienced in the past two weeks. There was so much to think about.

I recalled that on this very day sixty years ago German soldiers effortlessly opened the border crossing gates to drive their armoured columns across the hills and forests of Czechoslovakia. The well armed and disciplined Czech soldiers had been withdrawn from their virtually impregnable fortifications to a new boundary deep within the Czech territory where there were no natural barriers to protect their much diminished nation. In cities and villages, some Sudetens wildly welcomed the German troops who had come to "free them from Czech oppression." At the same time thousands of other Sudetens–their social democratic fellow citizens–were fleeing the area. Many were turned back by the Czech border guards into the hands of their enemies. I and my parents and some of my fellow passengers on this plane were successful refugees.

We had gone on a kind of pilgrimage before attending the Day of Recollection which was held in the small Bavarian city of Straubing. A previously suggested venue for this meeting was the city of Passau on the Austrian German border, however, it had to be changed because a meeting of neo-Nazis was scheduled for that city. It was felt that the Sudetens and the neo-Nazis could not comfortably coexist in so small a place; they were after all, our natural enemies.

On arrival in Munich, a bus took us to our hotel in the city of Dachau, a short distance north. The annual Octoberfest had taken up all the hotel accommodation available in the area: indeed, we were fortunate to be able to be housed in any locality so close to this annual beer binge.

The name Dachau, however, had for many of us a rather sinister connotation. Sixty years ago "going to Dachau" meant being shipped off to the infamous concentration camp which Hitler had set up shortly after his accession to power in 1933. It was to this institution that he had gathered his opponents for "concentration." In the fall of 1938, many Sudetens entered the gates of Dachau concentration camp under the sign *Arbeit Macht Frei* (Work Liberates) to be starved, tortured, overworked or used as guinea pigs in "medical research."

Shortly after arriving at Dachau, the mayor of the city came to our first meal to welcome us. In his speech he made reference to Dachau's negative history but endeavored to show us a more positive side. Indeed, after the war, he told us, when the Sudetens were expelled from Czechoslovakia many came to this area and were housed in the very barracks that had once been the prison camp. I wondered how they must have felt, but I suppose "any port in a storm" applied to their desperate situation. Nevertheless, they came to feel at home here for a large number remained in the vicinity. As we moved about in Dachau we noticed streets that were named after the communities from which the Sudetens had come, such as Reichenberg and Trautenau and other familiar names.

We were to return here and visit the site of the former concentration camp before our return to Canada. In the meantime we had scheduled a tour to our former homeland. Thus, after recuperating from jet lag, we boarded a beautiful, new Mercedes Benz bus. Twenty-five other former Sudetens mostly from Bavaria joined us on our tour. Together we set out for our first destination, Vienna.

One might well ask, why the Austrian capital? Vienna is best known for its music both the classical compositions of Mozart and Strauss but also the "Schrammel Music" played in the coffee houses or the more popular songs sung in a dialect incomprehensible to the non-Viennese in the new wine pubs of Grinzing and Nussdorf. Tourists from all over the world come to this beautiful and historic city on the "not so blue" Danube, to go to the Wiener Staatsoper and the Volksoper, or to see the famous Spanish Riding Academy. They come to taste the wonderful torten and Kafe mit Schlag. What most of these visitors do not know is that Vienna was a city that in spite of its aristocratic background was also the soil out of which modern social democracy had grown.

Vienna was a workers' city. My father was born on *Arbeitergasse* (Worker Street) and there was no shame in that. The modern Vienna has had many social democratic mayors and its council has done much to provide affordable housing in co-operatives for workers and retired people. In the latter days of the Hapsburg monarchy its parliament struggled against the conservatism of much of the rest of the empire. The *Seliger Gemeinde*, the Sudeten German Social Democratic Organization, bears the name of a political activist from Vienna.

We were returning to our ideological roots. Hubert Pfoch the former deputy mayor of Vienna, an energetic little man with a great sense of humour, met us and became our guide. We were taken on a tour of the city and had pointed out to us the housing co-operatives particularly the Karl Marx Court, one of the largest housing complexes which is highly rated by its residents. There is hardly ever a vacancy there. Nevertheless my Canadian travelling companions admitted that they preferred their single family homes across the ocean. Of course we attended a Heuriger, a new wine restaurant, where we joined in the singing and joviality which is a Viennese tradition.

Our hotel, the *Schloss am Wilhelminenberg*, is a large beautiful building located in the district of Ottakringen. Set on a hill on whose slopes grow the grapes that produce the new wine we drank, it overlooks the city. I admit that I got somewhat emotional as I looked down on the lights of Vienna on my way home from a little pub where a few of us had a foretaste of the party to take place next night. It occurred to me that somewhere down there in that city almost a hundred years ago, my father was born. The following day I took an hour off from my group and with the help of a taxi driver, another refugee who had fled from Iran six years ago, found the old apartment building. I must have raised some questions in the minds of any observers as I photographed this nondescript, three-storey building that had been my father's first home.

We concluded our stay in Vienna at the Prater, the famous amusement park with its giant ferris wheel from which I was able to get one last look at the city that features so prominently in the history of my family. After a lunch of enormous barbecued pork hocks irrigated by large steins of Viennese beer we once again boarded our bus and in little more than an hour pulled up before the gate festooned with the familiar red, white and blue flag. Before us was not Czechoslovakia but the Czech Republic, having separated from Slovakia a few years ago in a non-violent manner, a truly unusual phenomenon in modern political history.

Our first destination was the city of Brno. It used to be better known as Bruenn when it was virtually a German city. However, as I described earlier, on the morning of 30 May 1945, all Germans were ordered to gather on the square in the centre of town to be marched off in the direction of Austria. That was the end of its Germanness. During the communist era (1948-89), Brno had declined but since then the economy of the area has taken off with new technological industries creating employment and commerce.

We were taken to the very modern International Hotel near the centre of the old city. Here we were met by an elderly but most energetic woman, Dora Mueller, president of the German cultural organization. She was determined to keep the memory of Brno's German roots alive by giving courses in the German language and cultural history. There is not much about Brno that Dora doesn't know. She took us on a walking tour of the inner city, the old town, and then by bus through other parts of the city. Dora was often exasperated that our giant bus just couldn't penetrate the narrow, car clogged alleys that contained historic gems she wanted us to see.

Dora is also very interested in biology. She took us to the Mendeleum, the Augustinian monastery where in the middle of the nineteenth century the monk, Johannes Mendel, conducted experiments with sweet peas and developed the basics of the science of genetics. We were taken on a tour of this museum and the garden where his statue stands. At the opposite end of the small park is a stone monument erected only three years ago in memory of the Germans who were deported. I doubt that many of the visitors to the Mendeleum take notice of this marker that is inscribed in both German and Czech and refers to the injustice that was committed and pleads that never again will people be uprooted. She also pointed out the grassy area in front of a church nearby where on that fateful day all German people were assembled. Dora and her family were sufficiently Czech to have been allowed to remain in Brno although she vividly remembers that dreadful day.

Later, on my own, I walked to the railway station where on 7 November 1938 my father spent his last night in the republic. He and his group had come here from Prague on the long roundabout journey to Britain and were to change trains. However they missed their connection and had to spend the night in the station waiting room. Shortly before my departure for Germany I had discovered among my father's diaries an account of his journey to Britain. It was written on some sheets of paper torn out of a scribbler in which he tells of that night. I had some problem reading his handwriting, nevertheless, I came up with a printed account of that seven day journey to Britain.

The next leg of our trip took us to Prague. En route I read my father's account over the public address system of the bus which all found most poignant. There were some with us who remembered my father, among them Olga Sippl the woman who had organized this tour. Olga is a powerful and dedicated social democrat who gives leadership to the Seliger Organization in Bavaria. "One can hear the marks of your father's journalistic background in the words you read to us," she commented to me.

On the horizon appeared the gray line of apartment buildings that were constructed by the communist government on the outskirts of Prague. Among them was the Hotel Opatov where we were to be located for the next two days. It, and indeed the whole area, reminded me of the buildings I had seen in many of the cities in the former East Germany. The hotel room was comfortable enough but the hallways were drab and institutional. At night the sounds coming from outside indicated that this was not a quiet residential neighbourhood. Indeed, several of our rooms were broken into and a video camera and money were stolen.

In Prague we were met by Jan Hon, a gray bearded, academic looking man who is an official in President Václav Havel's office. He and several of his colleagues escorted us to the "Burg," the official residence of the president of the Czech Republic which overlooks the city. A tour of the castle had been arranged but two of us were not in the mood to walk through magnificent chambers, we were too anxious to experience the city and instead walked down the long steps from Hradčany Castle and across the Charles Bridge. It was a beautiful clear day and the Moldau shimmered in the sunlight. The saints looked down from their bridge piers as I remembered them from those days when Mother and I wandered the city sixty years ago.

We retraced our steps to the top of the hill and entered St. Vitus Cathedral. I looked about for the entrance to the

259

crypts where I had gone on that occasion which I described earlier in this book. The sun shone through the beautiful stained glass windows as it did then. I recognized so many familiar places and experienced once more an impatience to finish this chronicle that is now almost at its end. "This is a political tour group. We are not here merely to see the astrological clock on the old city hall but to experience the city as we had left it." So remarked Olga Sippl at the Narodny Dum, the headquarters of the Czech Social Democrats. We had been invited to meet with Dr. Miloš Bártha, the director of the Masaryk Academy and several members of parliament to hear something about the political situation in the country but also to dialogue with them about our own concerns. On the wall facing us was the familiar picture of Thomas Garrygue Masaryk, the philosopher king, founder and first president of Czechoslovakia. It was this same picture that I had seen in the many windows of the city when I made my first visit back in the Prague Spring of 1968.

The discussion turned out to be quite frank. Our tour leader Fred Kittel told of his own experiences. During the war he had joined the Czech Foreign Legion in Britain and fought for the liberation of Czechoslovakia from the Nazis. After the war he had a rather bitter experience. As long as he wore his uniform he was considered a "Ceskoslovenska Legionar" but as soon as he donned civilian clothes he was marked as a *Nemezki* (a German). His treatment was so bad that he decided to return to Britain and later on to Canada. He inquired about compensation paid out to the legionnaires, underlining that he was not here to beg for a pension but rather to find some sign of recognition of the efforts of his German speaking colleagues on behalf of the Czech state. His enquiry was taken very seriously by our hosts.

The discussion inevitably touched on the Beneš Decrees and the injustice that has not been resolved. "The

Czech Social Democrats need to have a greater sense of solidarity with social democrats in neighbouring Germany and indeed the world over," one of our group asserted, "and must give signs of a willingness to deal with those injustices." It is obvious that this is a serious and delicate matter for the Czech deputies. Among the Czech populace there is no great desire to revisit this issue, especially among the younger generation for whom economic matters are of greater concern.

Prague, in spite of the fact that I do not speak Czech, has about it a warm familiarity. My new friend, a kindred spirit, and I walked a great deal alone. We were not in the mood to be herded about in a large tour group. We ambled along the Moldau and sat for a few moments on the very benches where sixty years ago my mother and I had sat while studying English to ready ourselves for the trip abroad. We visited the old Jewish cemetery, my friend is Jewish. On Wenzeslaus Square we saw the memorial to Jan Palach who immolated himself after the tragic ending of the Prague Spring.

We came upon an exhibition of press photographs where we saw some gruesome pictures of war, repression and poverty that had been taken in the past few years and marveled at the courage and perception of those photographers. My friend remarked to me, "All this after two thousand years of Christianity." What could I say in response? I curbed my urge to defend the faith and wondered whether in fact the founder of that faith might not have made the same remark.

Our group, along with our Czech hosts, met for supper at the restaurant on the newly built television tower. From there one can see the whole of this wonderful and historic city. We saw it change from daylight through dusk to night. The lights of the city came on slowly as darkness descended until it seemed we were suspended above a marvelous chandelier. Next morning our bus took us out of the city once again and I, of course, wondered if and when and under what circumstances I would see this place again. I hoped that someday I might introduce it to my son and daughter as I have done for Marlene, my spouse.

❊   ❊   ❊

Indeed, two years later, I had the privilege of introducing my son, Stephen, to my birthplace. An educator and world traveller, Stephen was anxious to see the setting of so many stories about my past. We spent several days in Ústí nad labem: walking the city and visiting the Catholic Church with the leaning tower, the former Lutheran Church where my father was confirmed, my school and the house where I lived for the first nine years of my life.

One morning, we were caught in a heavy rainstorm and took shelter under a large chestnut tree. Suddenly, the rain stopped and blue sky appeared above us. As I looked across the street, I saw a large old house that looked familiar.

"You know, Stephen," I said, "I think that is the maternity hospital where I was born. I'm not absolutely sure, but I know it must be in this area."

"Well then, stand up on the steps and I'll take your picture," Stephen offered. As I posed, a man came down the steps of the house. He asked what was so interesting about this place. He told us it was a residence for homeless men and that several years ago it had been a maternity hospital.

"Yes," I replied. "Seventy-one years ago, I first saw the light of day in that building." He welcomed us inside and took us on a tour. It was nothing special, a long corridor with rooms on each side. Everything was painted an institutional green. We met a group of young women–volunteers and social workers–in the office and told them of my connection with the building. They gave us a round of applause. I told them that within these walls, I had first exercised my vocal chords. Stephen added that I haven't stopped since.

In a common room, we met some of the residents who were watching television. On hearing we were from Canada, one of the men raised his thumb in the air and shouted, "Toronto Maple Leafs."

Later, a chance encounter with the city archivist, Dr. Vladimir Kaiser got me a copy of my birth certificate which we had left behind when we fled in 1938. Dr. Kaiser's wife is a professor of modern history at the local university. She took us to the offices of her institute which to my astonishment were located one floor above what used to be Oma's apartment.

It is difficult for Stephen to comprehend that Ústí was once a predominantly German city, that a majority of its residents were expelled in the year after the war ended. As the guidebook states, there is nothing remarkable or picturesque about Ústí, however the surrounding countryside and the Elbe River valley are very beautiful indeed.

❖   ❖   ❖

We drove in a northerly direction towards the industrial and heavily polluted area that used to be my home. Our bus skirted the brown coal mining district near Kommotau. At a rest stop I managed to take a picture of several large cooling towers of a power plant shrouded in smoke and haze, not a nice scene to photograph. Some Romanis (gypsies) sat by the roadside selling mushrooms which they had picked in the nearby woods. We wondered about the quality of the fungi, exposed as they are to the chemical rich fog that descends on this countryside.

Soon after resuming our journey the highway encountered a rapidly flowing stream, the Eger River. We were now entering the well-known Egerland. In the distance we were able to see the Giant Mountains from where many of my Sudeten friends had come. A distinctive German dialect is spoken here which I have difficulty understanding but nevertheless sounds "down home" to me. The road was now lined with trees rich in fall colours that reminded me of my Canadian home. We entered the famous spa, Karlsbad, or Karlovy Vary as it is presently known.

The bus rolled past the suburbs and then wound its way through the wooded valleys. Palatial hotels surrounded by parks appeared more frequently as we neared the centre of the spa. Our bus pulled up in front of the Grand Hotel Pupp, one of the finest and best known of the Kuhr hostelries. A small river runs through the middle of the town and on either side streets are lined with small restaurants, cafes and boutiques.

As I got out of the bus I immediately noted the fresh, unpolluted air. It and the relaxed atmosphere gave me a lift especially after having just been through the other extreme closer to my former home. After checking into our rooms we set out in small groups to enjoy the sights of the city. Two of us elected to take the inclined railway to the top of one of the highest hills and then walked through the autumn foliage to an observation tower. From there we were able to see the rolling hills and the streets of the city that followed a small river. I picked up several crimson maple leaves which reminded me of home across the ocean. On our way down we followed the footpaths that crisscrossed through the pleasant woods.

Emma, one of our group who grew up in this city, took several of us for a personalized tour showing us the springs where people come to drink of the water that has been known for centuries for its curative effects. The nobility of Europe came regularly to this spa and its mineral water is exported throughout the world. The water is free, people bring their own special jugs to fill at the spouts and then sit on benches to sip it. There also are baths where patients come for the "cure." A sense of peace pervades this place. There is music in the air. Bands and Kurorchestras play on the squares before the spa halls and in the parks by the hotels.

What amazed me as I took in this city was the fact that once upon a time, until fifty-three years ago, it was largely German. The porcelain and glass factories that we visited had been staffed mostly by German craftsmen. Within a matter of less than two years virtually everything had changed. Most of the Germans were gone, transported one way or another across the border to Germany. Still many of the old Egerlander traditions are carried on. Some of us gathered at the Egerlander Hof for supper where an accordion player entertained. He knew well the songs that were so familiar to many of us and we joined in the singing. Egerlander anecdotes were shared among the group. For a few moments it seemed as though nothing had changed over the years that had gone by. That evening our people proved that although all were at least fifty-five and most over sixty-five, the oldest eighty-nine, they could still dance waltzes, polkas and even do the tango. I guess it's true that you can take the people out of the country but you can't take the country out of the people.

We were approaching the end of our sojourn in the Czech Republic. On our way towards the German border we stopped for lunch at Marienbad, another, smaller spa city. We were just in time to observe the wonderful fountain whose changing streams of water accompany the music that is played over the loudspeaker system. Each day at eleven a performance is given. We heard the overture to *Die Fledermaus* by Johann Strauss, music that is so typically Viennese, it evoked memories of the Austrian ethos of Bohemia. I thought of Otto Loeie on the CBC who speaks

265

with a distinctive Prague German accent as he presents the program "The Transcontinental." He often plays the music and tells the stories that are deeply imbued with the culture of this area of Europe.

Our driver, Gerhardt thought he knew a short cut to the border, but it didn't quite work out. Perhaps it was meant that we should drive through the *Boehmerwald* (Bohemian Forest). The road we were travelling wound through the forest and got narrower all the time. We saw people in the woods picking mushrooms. Then we approached a farm and a fork in the road beyond which the two roads became impossible for a large vehicle such as ours. A farm family was very curious and when our driver and several of our group armed with the road map approached they gathered around to give advice. Shortly the farmer himself took charge to give the definitive word on our geographic dilemma. He could not have been better cast for the role. He wore an old pair of faded green coveralls, rubber boots and a collarless shirt. A pair of glasses balanced at the end of his nose under which grew a thick unkempt gray mustache. I managed to photograph the "Four Power Conference" that took place on the roadside.

I could imagine the farmer saying that our bus of socialists had turned too far to the right. Taking the stance of a hockey referee ousting a player from the game he pointed back the way we had come. With unbelievable dexterity Gerhardt turned our bus around and we headed back to the place where we should have turned earlier. Soon we were at the German border. The red, white and blue flag was left behind, replaced by the red, gold and black. The Czech Republic with all its memories lay behind us.

In the distance as we drove south we saw the tower of the Regensburger cathedral. Our bus circled around that city, passed over the Danube and the Danube canal. By evening we approached the city of Straubing. As we entered we saw the familiar maple leaf flag flying among several others flags in front of the newly erected Josef von Frauenhofer Civic Centre where the International Friendship Meeting would be held the following day.

That day began downtown at the old city hall where the mayor of Straubing Reinhold Perlak welcomed us as well as some of the other guests. Among them were Georg Jaksch, son of the late Wenzel Jaksch the well-known leader of the Sudeten Social Democrats, and Volkmar Gabert the chair-person of the federal Seliger Gemeinde as well as delegates from the Czech Republic, some of whom we had already met in Prague, and many others.

It was a special day not only for us but for all of Germany, inasmuch as by the end of that day the people of this land would know who would be their new chancellor and what the constitution of the newly elected government would be. Most of our German participants had voted in the advance poll so they would not miss their democratic responsibility by attending this gathering. Indeed by early evening Helmut Kohl's long term in the office of Chancellor had ended to be replaced by Gerhardt Schroeder, a social democrat. There was much jubilation in our group.

Over five hundred people from Britain, Canada, Sweden, Germany and other countries assembled at eleven in the morning in the large hall of the civic centre. There was much conversation as old friends met around the tables. The Memorial Gathering began as Carolina Schmidt-Polex played an introduction on the harp. The hall fell silent.

After the opening welcome, Artur Schober an elderly gentleman with a shock of snow-white hair, chairperson of the Seliger Gemeinde of Baden-Wuertenberg, approached the microphone on the podium where the speakers were assembled. He recalled the tragic and triumphant history of the Sudeten social democratic movement. Others from Germany, Sweden, Britain, Austria, Canada and the Czech

Republic added their words and greetings. The International Friendship Meeting ended. Friends parted. There were feelings of nostalgia. Doubtless this will be the last occasion when so many old *Genossen und Genossinen* (comrades male and female) will meet. "We are getting older," was a commonly heard remark. The feelings and memories of these people can scarcely be described in words, hopefully my chronicle will have conveyed something of that sense.

A new generation with only a vague memory of the events of 1938 to 1945 has moved to centre stage. Hopefully they will not forget the fearless dedication of people in those small places such as Graupen or Trautenau, who stood defiantly as members of the Republican Guard against the Henlein thugs, or served as shop stewards, union leaders, editors, Red Falcon youth leaders and in many other positions that endangered their lives. Will the readers of twentieth century history be made aware of one of the largest ethnic cleansings with its bloody pogroms such as the Death March of Bruenn and the Massacre of Aussig? Will there be some record of the contribution Sudetens have made in the lands to which they were transplanted, of Henry Weisbach's leadership in the Canadian Labour Congress or Willi Wanka's community leadership in the Dawson Creek area of British Columbia? Will it be recognized that Bob Weil was one of the pioneers of psychiatry in Canada? One could go on. (There are some sad indications that the Sudetens' immigration has been forgotten. There is no mention of the arrival of the first group at Pier 21 in Halifax. As well *MacLean's* magazine in an article about the contribution of immigrants to Canada ignored the role of the Sudetens.) Wherever the Sudeten people have settled, in Sweden, in Britain and of course most predominantly in Germany where Wenzel Jaksch and Volkmar Gabert gave not only national but international leadership, significant contributions have been made. On the last day before we returned home, our Canadian group went to the memorial place of the former Dachau concentration camp. On my various trips to Germany, I have avoided going there but this was the time to go in the company of those who have some personal acquaintance with the meaning of this awful place.

I walked down the gravel road flanked by barbed wire and observation towers and entered the yard of the camp where prisoners had been lined up for hours to be counted or tortured and executed in view of their comrades. For us it could not be merely a place of historic interest, it was too close to our psyches.

We gathered at the wall above which stands the wrought iron memorial to the inmates of Dachau, a melange of what appears to be emaciated limbs in agonizing postures. A wreath was placed there and we paused in silence. I remembered that we were the fortunate ones. My father who had found his name on the Nazi hit list would probably have stood on this very square with Franz Jany and Emil Arnberg and others who also successfully fled to the safety of Britain and Canada. I thought of Alois Ullman who had gotten away to Britain and then after the March 1939 take-over of the rest of Czechoslovakia decided to return. On arriving at the Prague airport he had been immediately arrested and transported to Dachau. He managed to survive and upon returning to Czechoslovakia fulfilled an important role in the organizing of the Antifa (Anti-Fascist) transports of Sudetens to Germany.

I was pleased to see the Dachau KZ Memorial has many visitors. School children come to learn about this dark period of German history, military cadets in their smart gray jackets and red berets filed past the exhibits of brutality, the evidence of "man's inhumanity to man." One would fervently hope that Dachau KZ would cause people to think and act to prevent dictatorships from coming to power once again. Unfortunately Hitler wasn't the last of his breed. There was Augusto Pinochet in Chile, Suharto in Indonesia, Slobodan Milosovicz in Yugoslavia, to name but three whose atrocities the world must not forget. Or perhaps one ought not remain ignorant of the so-called liberation efforts by bombing nations into the stone age. It has been a bloody century!

The negative is easily remembered. What about the positives, those who have made major contributions fighting for freedom and equality, for human rights and social responsibility, especially in this age of the multinational corporations who plunder the world and its people in order to amass ever greater fortunes?

Our plane wings its way across Europe and the Atlantic Ocean. Time stands still as the sun hovers just above the left wing of the jet for quite some time. By mid-afternoon the plane descends into Halifax International Airport. As we skim over the tree tops short of landing I behold the glory of the fall colours. We are home where new tasks await us, "to stand on guard" as the Canadian national anthem has it, to be a socially responsible people in a land where all too often we forget that, like our natural resources, humans are precious. Let us not abandon each other.

"Where is my home?" is the question asked by the Czech national anthem. Surely our home is this globe where much needs to be done to uphold human rights, to struggle for social justice and to strive to preserve peace and the integrity of all God's creation.

Bibliography

Abella, Irving and Troper, Harold, *None Is Too Many: Canada And The Jews Of Europe*, 3rd ed. Toronto: Lester Publishing, Toronto, 1991.

Amstaetter, Andrew, *Tomslake: History Of The Sudeten Germans In Canada*. Saanichton, B.C.: Hancock House Publishers Ltd., 1978.

Diplomaticus, *The Czechs And Their Minorities*. London: Thornton Butterworth, 1938.

Finkel, Alvin and Liebovitz, Clement, *The Chamberlain-Hitler Collusion*. Merlin Press: James-Lorimer & Co., 1997.

Luewenheim, Francis L., *Peace Or Appeasement? Hitler, Chamberlain and The Munich Crisis*. Boston: Houghton Mifflin Co., 1964.

Luža, Radomir, *The Transfer Of The Sudeten Germans: A Study of Czech-German Relations, 1933-1962*. New York: New York University Press, 1964.

Mamatey, Victor and Luža, Radomir, *History of the Czech Republic 1918-1948*. Princeton: Princeton University Press, 1973.

Mann, Golo, *Deutsche Geschichte des 19 und 20 Jahrhunderts*. Stuttgart: Deutscher Buecherbund, 1958.

McGillvray, Gillian, "Colonizing The Victims Of 'Peace In Our Time'" (The Canadian Railways and the Sudeten

Uprooted and Transplanted

German Social Democratic Refugees in Western Canada),
Honours Thesis, 1994, Dalhousie University, Halifax, N.S.
Sayers, Derek, *The Coast Of Bohemia, A Czech History*.
Princeton: Princeton University Press, 1998.
Schilling, Rita, *Sudeten In Saskatchewan, A Way To Be Free*.
Saskatoon: St. Walburg Sudeten German Club and
Saskatoon German Council Inc., 1989.
Seliger Archiv, *Menschen Im Exile*. Stuttgart: 1974.
Seliger-Gemeinde, Weg, *Leistung und Schicksal*.
Stuttgart: 1972.
Seliger-Gemeinde, *Wenzel Jaksch, Sucher und Kuender*,
redaction Karl Kern. Munich: Die Bruecke, 1967.
Shirer, William, *The Rise and Fall of the Third Reich*. New
York: Simon and Schuster, Little Brown & Company, 1984.
Shirer, William, *The Nightmare Years, 1930-1940*. New
York: Little Brown & Company, 1994.
Sudeten Deutsches Archiv, *Odsun, Die Vertreibung Der
Sudeten-deutschen*. Munich: 1995.
Umlauft, Franz Josef, *Aussig An Der Elbe, Schicksal Einer
Deutschen Stadt In Boehmen*. Hilfverein Aussig. Munich:
Bayreuth, 1960.
Wanka, William, *Opfer Des Friedens, Die Sudetensiedlungen
in Canada*. Munich: Langen Mueller, 1988.
Wieden, Fritz, *The Sudeten German Socialists in Canada: A
Socio-economic History of German Canadians: They Too Founded
Canada*, ed. Helling, Rudolf. A. Wiesbaden: Steiner, 1984.

Acknowledgements

Many people read the manuscript for this book and made suggestions and corrections. I am particularly grateful to Arnold Edinborough, my former professor of English Literature at Queen's University. In 1953, he assigned our class either to write an essay on the modern English novel or to write a short story. I chose the latter which he liked. It refused to leave my consciousness and forty eight years later became part of the chapter called "Settlers." I wish also to thank Katherine Ferguson, Mary Baxter for their careful reading, as well as Prof. Greer Anne Wenh-In Ng, Dr. Anne Squire, Dr. Robert and Stella Weil and Dr. James and Phyllis MacNeill for their enthusiam and support.

Most valuable and without whose hard work and faith in this project it could not have reached fruition, I wish to thank Maryann Thomas, the publisher of The Ginger Press, and my editor, Lori Ledingham, whose energy and commitment was a refreshing spring that renewed my spirit.

Above all, however, I am most deeply indebted to my family, to Karla and Stephen whose critical judgement I respect, and to Marlene my beloved partner in life who read and reread the manuscript with red pencil in hand. She has stood by me through my years of ministry and especially over the past three years as I sought to gather these memories into the form of a book.

To all these and many more, I wish to express my heartfelt thanks.

HELP HEAL THE WOUNDS

The twentieth century, the last in the previous millennium, was a turbulent time for many people the world over. The term "ethnic cleansing" was coined in those latter years to describe in a less than realistic way the expulsion of racial and national minorities from the countries in which they had come to feel at home. Nations such as Canada have become the new home for many who have been uprooted.

Canada itself contains people who have experienced alienation and displacement within our own borders. Our Aboriginal people have been uprooted from their traditional lands to make way for the European settlers which includes my family. Most First Nation people do not live in the small enclaves which we call "Indian Reserves" but have drifted to cities to look for employment and often to languish at the bottom of the economic ladder, the streets. Truly these are the uprooted whose transplants have not taken.

In the efforts to deprive them of their language, culture and land, they have suffered severe wounds and healing is necessary. Money by itself cannot heal, but money can facilitate the various healing processes. A Healing Fund has been established by the United Church of Canada who in 1986 offered an apology to the people of the First Nations who had been maligned by residential schools operated by our church as well as in other ways.

This denomination of which I have been a member and a minister has striven to right the wrongs that were committed over years of that twentieth century and before. It is for this reason that I have committed to donate a portion of the price of each copy of *Uprooted and Transplanted* to the Healing Fund of the United Church. I have done this in order that I, who also was uprooted and transplanted, may express some solidarity with those with whom I have come to live, into whose land I have struck my roots.

Thank you for reading this book and your contribution to this healing mission.

ABOUT THE AUTHOR

Larry Henry

Hanns F. Skoutajan was born in Czechoslovakia and came to Canada with his parents just prior to the Second World War. He was educated at Queen's University and Theological College in Kingston, Ontario, and did post-graduate studies in Christian Social Ethics at the University of Muenster in Germany.

He has served the church as chaplain at Dalhousie University in Halifax and as Immigration Chaplain at the ports of Halifax, St. John, Montreal and Quebec City. In 1960, he directed the United Church's World Refugee Year Committee. He has served as minister of several churches in Ontario and for sixteen years was the minister of St. James-Bond United Church in Toronto. He has also chaired the denomination's committee on the Church and International Affairs and was the first president of the Ontario Coalition for Public Education. In 1986, Queen's University honoured him with the degree, Doctor of Divinity.

Skoutajan retired in 1993 from Knox United Church in Owen Sound where he lives with his wife. They have two children, Karla and Stephen.